Conversations with Marketing Masters

Conversations with Marketing Masters

Laura Mazur and Louella Miles

John Wiley & Sons, Ltd

Other Wiley Editorial Offices

John Wiley & Sons Inc., 111 River Street, Hoboken, NJ 07030, USA

Jossey-Bass, 989 Market Street, San Francisco, CA 94103-1741, USA

Wiley-VCH Verlag GmbH, Boschstr. 12, D-69469 Weinheim, Germany

John Wiley & Sons Australia Ltd, 42 McDougall Street, Milton, Queensland 4064, Australia

John Wiley & Sons (Asia) Pte Ltd, 2 Clementi Loop #02-01, Jin Xing Distripark, Singapore 129809

John Wiley & Sons Canada Ltd, 6045 Freemont Blvd, Mississauga, ONT, L5R 4J3, Canada

Wiley also publishes its books in a variety of electronic formats. Some content that appears in print may not be available in electronic books.

Library of Congress Cataloging-in-Publication Data

Mazur, Laura.
  Conversations with marketing masters / Laura Mazur and Louella Miles.
     p.   cm.
  Includes bibliographical references and index.
  ISBN-13: 978-0-470-02591-8 (cloth : alk. paper)
  1. Marketing. 2. Marketing—Management. 3. Marketing personnel—Interviews.
I. Miles, Louella. II. Title.
  HF5415.M374 2007
  658.8—dc22

        2006036078

British Library Cataloguing in Publication Data

A catalogue record for this book is available from the British Library

ISBN: 13 978-0-470-02591-8 (HB)

Typeset in 11/15pt Goudy by SNP Best-set Typesetter Ltd., Hong Kong
Printed and bound in Great Britain by TJ International Ltd, Padstow, Cornwall, UK
This book is printed on acid-free paper responsibly manufactured from sustainable forestry in which at least two trees are planted for each one used for paper production.

To Maz and Mike

Contents

Acknowledgements

Apart from thanking our marketing masters for generously giving us their valuable time and thoughtful contributions, we also want to acknowledge the help we have received from their colleagues where appropriate. In no particular order, thanks very much to Ingrid Mifflin, who works with Regis McKenna, Laura Ries of Ries and Ries, Andrew Sexton of Wunderman, Elaine Shaffer and Cynthia Tang of Harvard Business School, Jennifer Smith of the Peppers and Rogers Group and Brady TenBrink of Agora, Inc.

We also send heartfelt thanks to Claire Plimmer, Jo Golesworthy, Samantha Hartley and Viv Wickham of John Wiley & Sons, Ltd, for their efforts and encouragement. Thanks, as well, to photographer Teena Taylor.

About the Authors

Laura Mazur is a business writer and partner in Writers 4 Management, a professional writing firm. She has been a business journalist since 1978 and was editor of the UK's *Marketing* magazine from 1986 to 1989. She has written for a range of publications, including a weekly column for *Marketing* magazine for five years, and is also the author of management guides on international marketing and communications published by the Economist Intelligence Unit and Financial Times Reports.

Since they formed Writers 4 Management in 2004, she and her business partner, Louella Miles, have worked with a range of organizations and individuals, including writing white papers, running writing training courses, and acting as ghost writers/editors on a number of books. An economics graduate of Smith College in the USA, she also has an MA from the University of London in Soviet Studies.

Louella Miles is a business writer, and Laura's partner in Writers 4 Management. She started in consumer journalism in 1976, with the Consumers' Association, before moving over to business writing in 1980. She was managing editor of *Marketing* magazine through the mid to late 1980s. Her portfolio includes management reports on topics as diverse as corporate reputation and sponsorship, published by *Management Today* and *International Marketing Reports* respectively. She has also, for the past seven years, edited a weekly media newsletter, and produces a range of titles on qualitative research.

Introduction

Marketing – this fascinating and sometimes infuriating discipline – has been the focus of much of our working life as business journalists and writers. We have charted its course from the excesses of the 1980s, when budgets were seemingly limitless, to the belt tightening of the 1990s, and now into the age of accountability. We have seen organizations place it at the very heart of strategy, or relegate it to producing brochures.

Yet, however it's been defined or perceived over the years, marketing as a subject has never been less than absorbing. It has been our experience that those people who gravitate towards it, whether as practitioners, consultants and/or educationalists, are interested in people and interesting *as* people.

That's why, over the past few years, we had begun to wonder about how and why the biggest names in the field decided to devote their lives to its study and practice rather than another, perhaps less controversial, subject. So we set about compiling a list of people who have become so closely intertwined with marketing in general or a particular aspect of it. What, we wondered, makes them tick? How did they get to where they are? And what are their current views of marketing's health?

Those we chose are obvious. The list is, of course, by no means definitive. A few more could have been included. Sadly, in the case of Theodore Levitt, death intervened. Then there were those who, for one reason or another, were unable to take part. Never mind, because we are thrilled with the people we have included and found interviewing them stimulating and compelling. We have structured them as free-flowing conversations because we want to let their personalities shine through, without our getting in the way.

Even though our marketing masters are a diverse group of people, there are some common themes. There are worries about marketers and whether they have the ability to raise their game enough to make chief executives (CEOs) understand just how critical marketing is at a time when people power has moved from fiction to a fact of life. Other topics include the impact of technology on relationships, the power of buyers and the inexorable rise of the Chinese. All these indicate that there is never a dull moment when it comes to marketing.

A word about organization. We thought long and hard about the order because we didn't want to make any judgements about ranking. Then the answer seemed straightforward. As the founding father of marketing, and the one whom others often mention, we would put Philip Kotler first as *primus inter pares*. The rest are alphabetical.

The conversations are in three parts. First, we asked them questions about the professional journey they have taken. Then we delved into their current views of marketing. Finally, we got a bit more personal to find out what makes them tick.

An important point to make is that, while their names are all closely linked with the particular area they have pioneered, none of them has stood still. All are continually engaging with new ideas and new concepts to keep marketing relevant and pertinent.

Finally, the list of publications is necessarily selective. We have organized them from the newest to oldest, although in many cases the books have been reprinted many times over the years.

We feel privileged to have spent time with our marketing masters. We hope you enjoy getting to know them too.

1

....

Philip Kotler

The founding father

Philip Kotler is the S.C. Johnson & Son Distinguished Professor of International Marketing at the Kellogg School of Management, Northwestern University, Evanston, Illinois. He received his master's degree at the University of Chicago and his PhD Degree at Massachusetts Institute of Technology (MIT), both in economics. He did postdoctoral work in mathematics at Harvard University and in behavioural science at the University of Chicago.

Kotler is the author of Marketing Management: Analysis, Planning, Implementation and Control, *the most widely used marketing book in graduate business schools worldwide;* Principles of Marketing; Marketing Models; Strategic Marketing for Nonprofit Organizations; The New Competition; High Visibility; Social Marketing; Marketing Places; Marketing for Congregations; Marketing for Hospitality and Tourism; The Marketing of Nations; Kotler on Marketing; Building Global Biobrands; Attracting Investors; Ten Deadly Marketing Sins; Marketing Moves; Corporate Social Responsibility; Lateral Marketing *and* Marketing Insights from A to Z. *He has published over 100 articles in leading journals, several of which have received best-article awards.*

He was the first recipient of the American Marketing Association's (AMA) 'Distinguished Marketing Educator Award' (1985). The European Association of Marketing Consultants and Sales Trainers awarded Kotler its prize for 'Marketing Excellence'.

He was chosen as the 'Leader in Marketing Thought' by the Academic Members of the AMA in a 1975 survey. He also received the 1978 'Paul Converse Award' of the AMA, honouring his original contribution to marketing. In 1989, he received the Annual Charles Coolidge Parlin Marketing Research Award. In 1995, the Sales and Marketing Executives International (SMEI) named him 'Marketer of the Year'.

He has consulted for such companies as IBM, General Electric, AT&T, Honeywell, Bank of America, Merck and others in the areas of marketing strategy and planning, marketing organization and international marketing.

He has been Chairman of the College of Marketing of the Institute of Management Sciences, a director of the American Marketing Association, a trustee of the Marketing Science Institute, a director of the MAC Group, a former member of the Yankelovich Advisory Board, and a member of the Copernicus Advisory Board. He has been a trustee of the Board of Governors of the School of the Art Institute of Chicago and a member of the Advisory Board of the Drucker Foundation. He has received honorary doctoral degrees from Stockholm University,

University of Zurich, Athens University of Economics and Business, DePaul University, the Cracow School of Business and Economics, Groupe H.E.C. in Paris, the University of Economics and Business Administration in Vienna, Budapest University of Economic Science and Public Administration, and the Catholic University of Santo Domingo.

He has travelled extensively throughout Europe, Asia and South America, advising and lecturing to many companies about how to apply sound economic and marketing science principles to increase their competitiveness. He has also advised governments on how to develop stronger public agencies to further the development of the nation's economic well-being.

The professional journey

What, in your view, are you most famous for? This might seem an almost impossible question considering your career, but are there a few particular areas you feel are inextricably linked with your name?

My name is closely linked with the discipline of marketing. When I first examined marketing textbooks in the 1960s, I was appalled by their descriptiveness and lack of theory. They contained lists of the traits of good salespeople, the role of warehouses, a description of consumer demographics, and other definitions and lists. This was market anatomy but not market physiology.

I wanted to offer a different view of marketing and wrote my first book, *Marketing Management*, in 1967. It differed from previous books by applying economic, behavioural, organizational and mathematical theory to show how markets work and how marketing mix tools work.

Subsequently I introduced new concepts such as demarketing, social marketing, societal marketing and megamarketing. I also broadened marketing to include the marketing of persons, places, ideas, causes and organizations.

What was your thinking behind your first book?

I think part of the breakthrough was that I hadn't worked enough in marketing to develop a conventional mindset about marketing. I wanted to understand it better and, coming to the subject with a training in economics, organizational theory and social sciences, I felt that the books at the time were devoid of any scientific basis, or of any effort to focus on decision-making and marketing strategy.

I had already done a lot of work on game theory and decision trees and Markov processes and none of that was there. Yet I knew that marketing was really a set of decisions that would affect demand and revenue. And so, in writing *Marketing Management: Analysis, Planning and Control*, I would put marketing on a more systematic and scientific foundation. I was surprised and very pleased with the success of the book.

What else was around at the time?

Jerry McCarthy's book was the most popular one at the time. It was called *Basic Marketing*. Jerry had introduced a '4Ps' framework. He'd studied with Professor Richard Clewett at Kellogg, who talked about product, price, promotion and distribution. Jerry renamed distribution as place. Most other books talked a lot about distribution channels, sales force, price and advertising but Jerry offered a useful framework.

How did you start getting involved with marketing as a discipline?

I am trained as an economist. I studied under Milton Friedman at the University of Chicago for my MBA and emerged as a free market thinker. Then I studied under Paul Samuelson and Robert Solow at MIT and went Keynesian. All three won Nobel Prizes in economic science. But I found their explanations too simplified in terms of marketplace real phenomena. I always wanted to understand how people spent their money and made their choices.

To say that consumers make product choices that would maximize their utility doesn't say much. To say that producers make product and production choices to maximize their profits doesn't say much. Economists focus very much on prices and much less on other strong influences on demand such as advertising and personal selling. Economists ignore the complicated distribution system through which many products pass and where prices are set at different stages as the product passes from the manufacturer to the distributor to the dealers. I have great respect for the effort of economists to theorize but they do this by oversimplifying the complex dynamics of the actual marketplace and players. I believe that marketing is part of economics and enriches economic theory.

I became enamoured of several marketing questions, such as how many sales persons should a firm hire, what is the best way to compensate them, how to determine how much to spend on advertising, and other questions. When I was offered a position at Northwestern University in 1962 to teach marketing, I decided that this was the opportunity to address the questions that had been haunting me in economics.

My active involvement in marketing had actually started a year before joining Northwestern. I had been selected as one of 50 business school professors to spend a year at Harvard in a Ford Foundation program to study higher mathematics as they apply to making better business decisions. The 50 participants fell into some natural groupings: professors of accounting, of finance, of manufacturing, of marketing, etc. I fell in with the marketing group that included such people as Frank Bass, Edgar Pessemier, Jerry McCarthy and Robert Buzzell. The group worked on applying the mathematics they were learning to marketing decisions and I participated. The contrast between this quantitative approach and the normal textbooks in marketing was extreme.

This was a period of gestation for me. One of the persons whom I worked with in this program, Donald Jacobs, was one of the 50 and when he went back to his university, Northwestern, he told his colleagues that he had spotted me in the group and that they should recruit me. They interviewed me and hired me. I was given a choice to teach either managerial economics or marketing at Northwestern in 1962.

Don advised me to teach marketing on the grounds that managerial economics was a well-settled field but marketing was in a bad state and provided a lot of room for new theory. He had the feeling that with my theoretical cast of mind I could make a fresh contribution to marketing. So this was the triggering event. Don went on to become the visionary dean of Kellogg and his 25-year tenure led us to become one of the leading business schools in the nation.

What had you been doing before joining Northwestern?

I was teaching managerial economics, not marketing, at Roosevelt University in Chicago. I had wanted to stay in Chicago because of family.

Roosevelt University, which was started in 1946 after the war, was named after Franklin D. Roosevelt. It was a very interesting and seminal place because a lot of the faculty were eminent scholars who had fled Europe and needed a place to work. Roosevelt University hired them. I was there for about four years and then the Northwestern opportunity came along and I decided to move there.

Why do you think your ideas have caught on and become the basis of modern marketing?

After publishing the first edition of *Marketing Management* in 1967, I received a great amount of positive feedback to the effect that I had put marketing on a more scientific and decision-making basis. This was amplified a few years later when I published *Marketing Decision Making: A Model Building Approach*. Shortly thereafter I published a series of articles in the *Journal of Marketing*, three of which were voted the best article of the year in their respective years.

This was followed by eight articles published in the *Harvard Business Review* over several years that increased my visibility among practitioners. I had also added consulting to major companies and alerted them to the need to segment, target and position better and to become customer-centric. I would guess that by 1975 my reputation was well established.

And when did you begin to realize that you were becoming a name that was resonating all over the world?

I didn't consciously use marketing to market my ideas. They spread without assistance. *Marketing Management* became the gold standard throughout the world. When I meet managers in China, India, Germany, Brazil and elsewhere, it seems that they all studied marketing with my book. Today *Marketing Management* is in its 12th edition and *Principles of Marketing* is in its 11th edition. I did a lot of speaking at academic, corporate and public events and published a lot of papers and this contributed to the interest in my ideas.

I was invited to seminars and debates and put forth my strong views about what marketing should be. If you call that marketing my views, then yes, of course I did. But it wasn't like I had a Kotler brand development plan in mind. I did realize that I didn't want to just be in teaching – I wanted to be out there researching, writing and consulting. And that meant being not only in the USA but abroad. The opportunities came along to consult and teach in Europe, later in South America, and later still in Asia. I was becoming a brand largely by spreading my views.

How did organizations react initially to the ideas? Was there any resistance, and why, in your view?

My marketing management work was well received by marketing departments within companies. The marketers appreciated that their discipline was achieving more useful concepts, tools and scientific status, and that this would help them earn more respect from sales, finance, engineering and manufacturing. I worked hard to distinguish the role and contribution of the marketing people from the role and contribution of the sales people. In simple form, I said that marketers build demand and the brand, while the sales people get the orders.

You also broadened the concept of marketing and made what must have seemed like quite a radical leap into showing that marketing could be used in nonprofit organizations?

In the late 1960s, lifestyles were changing, the Vietnam War was going on and protest movements centering on social issues were flaring up.

I felt that marketers could contribute to positive social change. I began to think that some of the concepts such as segmentation, targeting and positioning could be used in broader areas than selling goods and service. So the times were one influence. My Kellogg colleagues, particularly Sidney Levy and Gerald Zaltman, were also joining in efforts to broaden marketing beyond the domains of goods and services.

In the early 1970s I wrote *Strategic Marketing for Non-Profit Organizations* and showed how museums, performing arts organizations, churches, social welfare organizations and others could gain insight into their problems and improve their effectiveness by viewing their problems through the lens of marketing.

Later I wrote *Social Marketing* with Ned Roberto to show how cause organizations could market their causes more effectively, whether it is to say

'No' to hard drugs, to protect the environment, or to advocate better eating and more exercise.

What were the challenges you faced in getting these concepts accepted?

When I broadened marketing beyond goods and services, some older marketing academics challenged me on the grounds that marketing must involve payment for goods and services. But I said that nonprofit organizations could use marketing to segment their markets, choose the segments they want to serve and satisfy, create a differentiated position in the market space, and apply the 4Ps of product, price, place and promotion to create a desired behavioural response.

Your ideas have been seminal to the evolution of marketing. Has the message gotten through to the extent you hoped it would?

My main message continues to be that we must choose carefully the markets and market segments we want to serve and to create, communicate and deliver superior value. Our job is to build customer loyalty and trust by delivering on the promise made by our brand. Today many companies are preaching customer value and customer-centredness, although in many cases it is more talk than action.

I would like to dispel the myth that marketing contributes very little to long-running company success. Marketing has the potential not only to help sales sell more today but also to identify new opportunities and create new solutions and strategies. At the same time, management must recognize that marketing cannot work miracles, except occasionally! We have to be honest about what marketing can and cannot accomplish.

> *My main message continues to be that we must choose carefully the markets and market segments we want to serve and to create, communicate and deliver superior value. Our job is to build customer loyalty and trust by delivering on the promise made by our brand. Today many companies are preaching customer value and customer-centredness, although in many cases it is more talk than action.*

You obviously still enjoy teaching?

Yes, I enjoy talking to a class of students or managers. I welcome their questions. I learn from teaching. I can test theories in the classroom, distribute some new writing and get feedback.

When you get involved with a company, either directly or for the purposes of teaching, what are the first things you investigate to judge how effectively it carries out marketing?

I first ask to see a list of the company's market segments and marketing channels for reaching each of these segments. I also want to know how important they think each segment is and the criteria they use. Next I ask for the most recent study of consumer behaviour in each segment. I am not impressed if they give me a study that is more than two years old; customers change faster than that. Then I ask to see samples of current marketing plans. I am often astonished to find plans with insufficient data, weakly stated objectives, no strategy, a lot of miscellaneous tactics and poor controls.

How do you feel about being seen as the founding father of marketing?

I always say that I stand on the shoulders of giants. I am indebted to a number of deep thinkers for my work in marketing, including Peter Drucker, Theodore Levitt, John Howard, Herbert Simon, Dick Cyert and James March.

It is a responsibility to be thought of as someone who has pushed the field forward. Some scholars retire because other interests come up. I have many new interests but I continue to be fascinated with all the manifestations of marketing. I would get bored teaching geometry but am never bored with marketing.

I've always welcomed criticism and challenging alternative frameworks. If someone offers a really fresh view, or a new departure point, I would examine it as quickly as anyone else. And that has happened many times. It has happened when relationship thinking replaced transaction thinking; when customer lifetime value replaced customer current profitability; when services and experiences came to be as or more important than the product itself. So I am busy watching new developments in the field.

Current views of marketing

What are the current challenges marketing is facing?

People continue to confuse marketing with selling. I have to remind audiences that marketing is more than selling existing 'stuff'. Marketing starts long before there is a product and continues long after it is sold. Marketing is the tool for segmenting markets, discovering unmet needs, creating new solutions. Marketing, when done well, creates the company's future.

Another challenge is to find new ways to get messages and offerings to people who can benefit from them. Advertising has been a major force for reaching large audiences but its effectiveness, particularly the 30-second commercial, is declining. There is too much cluttering of messages, people are buying devices to avoid the messages, and are increasingly busy with other activities such as the internet, video games, emailing, etc. It is getting harder to catch 10 seconds of anyone's attention. Some consumers are avoiding ads like the plague. We may have to move to getting their permission to send a message.

Another challenge is that customers are more educated and have more market knowledge at their fingertips than ever before. They can look up on the internet the competitive features and prices found in any category they are interested in. To the extent that consumers perceive the products as similar, they will pay more attention to who is charging the lowest price. Marketers are thus challenged to differentiate their offerings in real or psychological terms.

Senior management is increasingly challenging the marketers to financially account for their impact. They and the chief financial officer want to know if marketing money is being spent productively.

How should marketing evolve to deal with this growing complexity?

Marketing departments need to upgrade their present skills and add new ones. The four traditional skills have been marketing research, advertising, sales promotion and sales management. Each of these is becoming more sophisticated. In addition, marketing departments have had to add newer skills such as direct mail, telemarketing, public relations, sponsorships, event management, e-marketing, and so on. Most people in a marketing department will work on *downstream marketing*, namely helping the sales force to sell more of the current products and services. The marketing department also needs some members to work on *upstream marketing*, to discover new markets and imagine new offerings.

Marketing departments should not hesitate to add highly skilled and specialized persons to their department. Persons skilled in datamining, model building and deep psychological analysis can add value to untangle complexity.

What should marketers themselves be doing to succeed in this climate?

Marketers will have to work harder and smarter. They had it easy when all they needed was a large budget to pay, spray and pray. Now they have to manage an exploding number of media, communication channels and distribution channels not only domestically but globally.

On top of this, senior management is pressing marketers to supply return on investment (ROI) measures of the impact of various marketing campaigns and activities. Marketers must learn the language of finance to account for their activities.

I actually prefer that persons who want to become brand marketers don't start their career in marketing. They should start their career in sales. They should get further experience in advertising, public relations, events and other tools. They should work in the customer service department, and also as team members in new product development projects.

Marketers will have to work harder and smarter. They had it easy when all they needed was a large budget to pay, spray and pray. Now they have to manage an exploding number of media, communication channels and distribution channels not only domestically but globally.

What about companies appointing chief marketing officers?

Multi-divisional companies are appointing chief marketing officers (CMOs) to review and improve the quality of marketing in the organization. The CMO locates at headquarters and in principle operates at the level of the other chief officers such as the chief financial officer (CFO), chief information officer (CIO), chief technology officer (CTO), etc. The CMO, in addition to upgrading the organization's marketing skills, also has responsibilities including helping strengthen corporate and individual brands, finding new product opportunities, and bringing the voice of the customer into senior management deliberations, This is a tall order.

What's your feeling about the rise of customer relationship management (CRM)? Can it help or is it a fad?

CRM is not a fad. The more we know about individual customers, the better we can serve them. We can recognize upselling and cross-selling opportunities. If we satisfy them more, we will retain them longer as customers. If we don't satisfy them, we lose them as customers. So we need a relational database to access customer information. Access to this database should be available to our salespeople, brand managers, market researchers, merchandisers and others. By doing datamining, we can spot new trends and new segments.

CRM did not work out well in every adopting company. One estimate held that 40% of the companies adopting CRM were disappointed. These were the companies which weren't ready for it and simply bought the promising tool because competitors were buying it. They were not sufficiently customer-centred companies. The tool did not get enough use. Now CRM is in a second stage where the sellers and the buyers are more sophisticated. CRM is being purchased more judiciously by companies which are ready to use it for gaining a competitive edge through knowing relatively more about their customers.

What distinguishes companies that are good at marketing from ones that are less successful?

Successful marketing companies are those which can innovate, launch and learn. Without investing in innovation and change, a company will eventually go under. Innovation requires an organization that wants to win and that focuses on target customers and their evolving needs. New product and service ideas are welcome and are, in fact, solicited from research and development, customers, dealers, the advertising agency and other stakeholders.

These companies know when to advance an attractive-looking idea and when to kill it. They use a stage gate method that screens out bad ideas early and lets great ideas go to launch. But the launch is done carefully with feedback collected continuously. The feedback will open the marketers' eyes to new problems and opportunities. The learnings might require marketers to revise tactics, strategies and even objectives.

Great marketing companies are able to visualize the evolution of the market offering. Starbucks didn't just stay a coffee retailer. It is retailing music in its stores. It is selling its products in supermarkets. It is found in dozens of countries. Apple's Steve Jobs didn't just launch an iPod to carry music. He visualized ahead of his competitors that it would evolve to carrying thousands of photos, and later videos. He is ready to cannibalize the earlier iPod versions before they have fully saturated the market in the interests of leading the competitors, rather than allowing them to lead in product evolution.

By contrast, losing companies fail to monitor new technologies, new lifestyles, new competitors. Car makers such as General Motors and Ford have had so much time to watch the Japanese, to learn from them, and yet were so slow at doing so. They answered the success of Japanese small cars in the 1970s by countering with small inferior cars. They were late in learning how to put more quality in a car. They are late in offering hybrid and new fuel-efficient engines. Failing companies operate bureaucratically and arrogantly. Instead of looking out of their windows, they look at their own image in a mirror.

What tips would you offer those struggling to reach marketing excellence?

Study the marketing skills and practices of high growth, high profit, highly respected and long-lasting firms. Read Harvard Business School cases on winners and losers in your industry. Read the business and marketing press. Read the new marketing books that are nominated by the American Marketing Association (AMA) as the best marketing books each year.

Getting more personal

What do you think it was about you as a person that made you decide that these concepts were so important to disseminate to a wider audience?

From the earliest times, I have wanted to work toward the improvement of human welfare. My choice of economics as my field of study was based on its potential to help improve the growth and distribution of wealth in society. Marketing, as a branch of economics, offered a rich set of tools and understandings about how markets work and how value can be created.

I began to see marketing as the ability to create, communicate and deliver value whether in commercial markets, nonprofit markets or even government markets. We can market goods, services, experiences, information, persons, places, ideas and causes. I have been on a mission to show audiences in my talks, consulting and writing how to create more value for those they intend to serve.

Marketing was defined many years ago as the 'art and science of raising standards of living'. Marketing uses the basic concepts of psychology, social psychology, sociology, anthropology, economics and organization theory to help 'engineer' solutions.

What are you proudest of in terms of your work?

Clarifying the role of marketing (as opposed to sales) and broadening the concept of marketing to help nonprofit and public organizations achieve their objectives. Why? Because I think marketing offers a powerful perspective on how to sense, serve and satisfy the needs of others.

Do you have what you would consider a defining moment in your life – one that set you on the path you eventually followed?

Growing up in a hard working-class family that valued education gave me a view of the world. I not only wanted to improve the quality of my life but also the lives of those who were less fortunate. My early years occurred during the Great Depression. People were poor and grabbing any jobs they could get. I felt that so many people were dealt a bad hand through no fault of their own. The presence of great wealth alongside great poverty always bothered me.

The late 1960s and early 1970s were a period of social ferment and activism. I threw myself into the period, wanting to contribute ideas on how to improve social conditions. I worked with Gerald Zaltman and Ira Kaufman to edit a book on social action, *Creating Social Change* (1972). Later I worked with my former student, Ned Roberto, to write *Social Marketing*, which addressed how to market social causes. Later Nancy Lee joined us to write a second edition. And she and I published *Corporate Social Responsibility: Doing the Most Good for Your Company and Your Cause*. I am currently working with Ned Roberto and Tony Leisner on a book on how to alleviate poverty through applying marketing theory and concepts. I guess that I keep returning to the 'do gooder'

The marketplace is endlessly fascinating. The stories and competitive battles read like a novel. There is a never-ending stream of new companies arising to serve markets in new ways . . . I know I wouldn't get the same kick from researching and teaching accounting.

nature of my personality. I know I wouldn't get the same kick from researching and teaching accounting.

You have talked about a long romance with marketing. What has kept it going?

The marketplace is endlessly fascinating. The stories and competitive battles read like a novel. There is a never-ending stream of new companies arising to serve markets in new ways. When patterns seemed set in the airline industry, along came Richard Branson with his Virgin Atlantic Airlines and Herb Kelleher with Southwest. When patterns seemed set in the furniture retailing industry, along came Ingvard Kamprad and Ikea.

Selected publications

Marketing in the Public Sector: A Roadmap for Improved Performance, Prentice Hall/Financial Times, 2007. Co-author: Nancy Lee.

Business to Business Brand Management, Springer, 2006. Co-author: Waldemar Pfoertsch.

The Elusive Fan: Reinventing Sports in a Crowded Marketplace, McGraw-Hill, 2006. Co-authors: Irving Rein and Ben Shields.

Marketing Places Latin America, Makron and Paidos, 2006. Co-authors: Irving Rein, Don Haider and David Gertner.

According to Kotler: The World's Foremost Authority on Marketing Answers All Your Questions, AMACOM, 2005.

Corporate Social Responsibility: Doing the Most Good for Your Company and Your Cause, John Wiley & Sons, Inc., 2005. Co-author: Nancy Lee.

Attracting Investors: A Marketing Approach to Finding Funds for Your Business, John Wiley & Sons, Inc., 2004. Co-authors: Hermawan Kartajaya and David Young.

Ten Deadly Marketing Sins: Signs and Solutions, John Wiley & Sons, Inc., 2004.

Lateral Marketing: A New Approach to Finding Product, Market, and Marketing Mix Ideas, John Wiley & Sons, Inc., 2003. Co-author: Fernando Trias de Bes.

Marketing Insights A to Z: 80 Concepts Every Manager Needs to Know, John Wiley & Sons, Inc., 2003.

Rethinking Marketing: Sustainable Marketing Enterprise in Asia, Prentice-Hall, 2003. Co-authors: Hermawan Kartajaya, Hooi Den Hua and Sandra Liu.

Marketing Global Biobrands: Taking Biotechnology to Market, The Free Press, 2003. Co-author: Françoise Simon.

Marketing Moves: A New Approach to Profits, Growth, and Renewal, Harvard Business School Press, 2002. Co-authors: Dipak C. Jain and Suvit Maesincee.

A Framework for Marketing Management, Prentice-Hall, 2001, 2003.

Marketing Asian Places, John Wiley & Sons, Inc., 2001. Co-authors: Michael Hamlin, Irving Rein and Donald Haider.

Repositioning Asia: From Bubble to Sustainable Economy, John Wiley & Sons, Inc., 2000. Co-author: Hermawan Kartajaya.

Marketing Places Europe, Financial Times, 1999. Co-authors: Christer Asplund, Irving Rein and Donald Haider.

Marketing Management – An Asian Perspective, Prentice-Hall, 1996, 1999, 2003, 2006. Co-authors: Swee Hoon Ang, Siew Meng Leong and Chin Tiong Tan.

Principles of Marketing – European edn, Prentice-Hall, 1996, 1999, 2001. Co-authors: Gary Armstrong, John Saunders and Veronica Wong.

Kotler on Marketing: How to Create, Win, and Dominate Markets, The Free Press, 1999.

Museum Strategies and Marketing: Designing the Mission, Building Audiences, Increasing Financial Resources, Jossey-Bass, 1998. Co-author: Neil Kotler.

The Marketing of Nations: A Strategic Approach to Building National Wealth, The Free Press, 1997. Co-authors: Somkid Jatusripitak and Suvit Maesincee.

Standing Room Only: Strategies for Marketing the Performing Arts, Harvard Business School Press, 1997. Co-author: Joanne Scheff.

Marketing for Hospitality and Tourism, Prentice-Hall, 1996, 1999, 2003, 2006. Co-authors: John Bowen and James Makens.

Marketing Places: Attracting Investment, Industry and Tourism to Cities, States and Nations, The Free Press, 1993. Co-authors: Irving Rein and Donald H. Haider.

Marketing for Congregations: Choosing to Serve People More Effectively, Abingdon Press, 1992. Co-authors: Norman Shawchuck, Bruce Wrenn, and Gustave Rath.

Social Marketing: Strategies for Changing Public Behavior, The Free Press, 1989. Co-author: Eduardo Roberto. 2nd edn: retitled *Social Marketing: Improving the Quality of Life* (co-authors: Ned Roberto and Nancy Lee), Sage, 2002.

High Visibility: The Making and Marketing of Professionals into Celebrities, Dodd, Mead & Co., 1987. Co-authors: Irving Rein and Martin Stoller. Re-published in a second edition by NTC, 1998. Re-published in a third edition by McGraw-Hill and called *High Visibility: Transforming Your Personal and Professional Brand* (co-authors: Irvin Rein and Michael Hamlin).

Marketing for Health Care Organizations, Prentice-Hall, 1987. Co-author: Roberta N. Clarke.

The New Competition: What Theory Z Didn't Talk About – Marketing, Prentice-Hall, 1985. Co-authors: Liam Fahey and Somkid Jatusripitak. Editions in Indonesian, German, Portuguese.

Strategic Marketing for Educational Institutions, Prentice-Hall, 1985, 1995. Co-author: Karen Fox.

Marketing Professional Services, Prentice-Hall, 1984, 2002. Co-author: Paul N. Bloom. 2nd edn (Co-authors Paul N. Bloom and Tom Hayes), 2002.

Marketing Essentials, Prentice-Hall, 1984. Renamed *Marketing – An Introduction*, Prentice-Hall, 1987, 1990, 1993, 1997, 2000, 2003, 2005, 2007, with co-author Gary Armstrong joining after the first edition. Many foreign editions.

Cases and Readings for Marketing for Nonprofit Organizations, Prentice-Hall, 1983. Co-authors: O.C. Ferrell and Charles Lamb. Renamed *Strategic Marketing for Nonprofit Organizations: Cases and Readings*.

Principles of Marketing, Prentice-Hall, 1980, 1983, 1986, 1989, 1991, 1994, 1996, 1999, 2001, 2004, 2006, With co-author Gary Armstrong joining starting in the 3rd edn. Many language editions.

Marketing for Nonprofit Organizations, Prentice-Hall, 1975, 1982, 1986, 1991, 1996, 2003. Editions in German and Dutch. Renamed *Strategic Marketing for Nonprofit Organizations* and published with co-author Alan Andreasen in 2006.

Creating Social Change, Holt, Rinehart & Winston, 1972. Co-editors: Gerald Zaltman and Ira Kaufman.

Simulation in the Social and Administrative Sciences, Prentice-Hall, 1972. Co-editors: Harold Guetzkow and Randall L. Schultz.

Readings in Marketing Management, Prentice-Hall, 1972, 1976, 1980, 1984. Co-editor: Keith Cox. Title changed to *Marketing Management and Strategy*, revised edn, 1983.

Marketing Decision Making: A Model Building Approach, Holt, Rinehart & Winston, 1971. Revised in 1983 and renamed *Marketing Models* and re-published by Harper & Row, with new co-author Gary L. Lilien. Editions in Spanish and French.

Revised in 1992 and re-published by Prentice-Hall with co-authors Gary L. Lilien
and K. Sridhar Moorthy.

Marketing Management, Prentice-Hall, 1967, 1971, 1976, 1980, 1984, 1988, 1991,
1994, 1997, 2000, 2003, 2006. Versions in French, German, Portuguese, Spanish,
Italian, Japanese, Russian, Chinese, Finnish, Indonesian, Turkish, Hebrew,
Slovenian, etc. At least six are adaptations, not just translations, with foreign
co-authors, bringing in relevant country cases, statistics and marketplace
descriptions.

2

....

David Aaker

Brand equity trailblazer

David A. Aaker is the Vice-Chairman of Prophet Brand Strategy and has been Professor Emeritus of Marketing Strategy at the Haas School of Business, UC Berkeley since 2000; E.T. Grether Professor of Marketing from 1994; J. Gary Shansby Professor of Marketing Strategy from 1981 to 1994; Professor, 1970 to 1981; Frankfurt Chamber Chair Visiting Professor, Goethe University, Frankfurt, April–May 1987; Visiting Professor, Aoyama Gakuin University, July 1991, Tokyo.

He is the winner of a number of career awards for contributions to the science of marketing, including the 1996 Paul D. Converse Award for outstanding contributions to the development of the science of marketing, the 2000 Vijay Mahajan Award for career contributions to marketing strategy, the 2004 Buck Weaver Award for the theory and practice of marketing and the 2005 Innovative Contributions to Marketing Award from the Marketing Management Association.

He has published over 100 articles and 13 books, including Strategic Market Management, Managing Brand Equity, Building Strong Brands, Brand Leadership (co-authored with Erich Joachimsthaler), Brand Portfolio Strategy and From Fargo to the World of Brands. His books have been translated into 18 languages.

He was named one of 30 leaders in the field of marketing thought in a University of Wisconsin survey, fall 1975, and one of the top 20 most cited marketing scholars from 1972 to 1975 by a Georgia State study. He was a Fellow at the World Economic Forum at Davos, 1999, 2000.

Cited as one of the most quoted authors in marketing, Aaker has won awards for the best article in the California Management Review and (twice) in the Journal of Marketing. A recognized authority on brand equity and brand strategy, he has been an active consultant and speaker throughout the world and is on the board of directors of California Casualty Insurance Company and The Food Bank of Contra Costa and Solano Counties. He has been an advisor to Dentsu Inc. since 2001.

The professional journey

After MIT, you started your career at Texas Instruments (TI) and along the way also had a go at starting your own firm. What made you change courses to academia?

I'd realized that my career at TI was doomed. I was a marketing person in an engineering and manufacturing company that didn't have a clue about marketing or marketing people and I was in Houston when the action was in Dallas. An attempt to run a small metal fabricating company on the side with two friends failed and made me appreciate the challenges of being an entrepreneur.

My escape route was a decision to enter Northwestern's four quarter MBA program. After only one quarter, I decided that I wanted to pursue a PhD because the life of a professor with its freedom, stimulation and the rewards from teaching seemed attractive. Luckily, Stanford accepted me into its PhD program only a few weeks before the fall term started – that would have never happened today.

What were your research interests at the outset of your career and how did they evolve?

I have had at least three overlapping research periods. During the first 12 years or so I was primarily a model builder and statistician because I liked it, had an aptitude towards it, and it was academically respectable. I developed brand choice models, media decision models and advertising response models, all fairly nerdy, and wrote books on advertising management and market research.

In the early 1980s I moved into strategy research, a subject I was interested in during my TI days. The most notable strategy research stream was a series of econometric studies with a Haas colleague, Bob Jacobson, now at the University of Washington. One article, which turned out to be visible and controversial, exploded the conventional wisdom of the day that the route to profitability was to increase market share. A desire to understand strategy from a multifunctional perspective then led me to write *Strategic Marketing Management*, now in its eighth edition.

The third phase, which began in the mid-1980s, focused on brands and brand strategy. My strategy writing and research convinced me that executives were too short-term-oriented, partly because of pressure to satisfy stock market investors who rely on quarterly earnings (and usually lack information about strategy) and partly to gain personal advancement by showing tangible results.

I came to believe executives needed to focus more attention on building and managing assets that will have a long-term payout. I decided to participate in this effort by encouraging executives to elevate brand assets in their priorities and to develop tools and methods to build and manage brands. My background in marketing research, advertising and strategy all turned out to be relevant to my new direction.

My research on brands started in 1986 with a series of studies with Kevin Keller, now at Dartmouth but then a new professor at the Haas School, with training in cognitive psychology from Duke University. The centrepiece of our work was an influential article in the *Journal of Marketing*, 'Consumer Evaluations of Brand Extensions', which looked at reactions to proposed extensions that varied as to brand fit. For example, McDonald's was conceptually extended into frozen fries, a theme park and photo processing. One finding was that perceived quality and credibility were key determinants of an extension's success.

Was your move into brands and brand strategy caused in part by the fact that branding was beginning to have far more resonance with senior management than marketing?

Yes, executives were realizing that many of their strategic issues involved problems or limitations with their brands and brand strategy. They became motivated to create stronger brands and more responsive brand portfolios. The most accepted lever of the day, simply to increase the advertising budget, was not achieving the results they were looking for. They needed a reason to take a different course – the concept of brand equity came into being at the right time.

The coining of the term brand equity was, from my biased judgement, one of the most significant events in marketing. Before brand equity, the task was to influence brand image and purchase decision by developing an advertising budget and delegating how it was spent to advertising people. After the concept of brand equity got traction, the perspective totally changed. Managing brands was then strate-

Before brand equity, the task was to influence brand image and purchase decision by developing an advertising budget and delegating how it was spent to advertising people. After the concept of brand equity got traction, the perspective totally changed. Managing brands was then strategic rather than tactical, got the attention of top executives, and required brand-building programs that involved the whole organization.

gic rather than tactical, got the attention of top executives, and required brand-building programs that involved the whole organization.

What was your role in popularizing brand equity?

In 1988, the Marketing Science Institute (MSI), a consortium of firms that fund academic research, sponsored its first conference around brands, stimulated in part because the MSI firms had determined that brand strategy should be a research priority of MSI. At that conference it became clear to me that this emerging field needed some structure and definition. As a result I wrote my first brand book, *Managing Brand Equity*, which was published by The Free Press in 1991.

One role of the book was to define brand equity – a set of assets and liabilities linked to the brand name and symbol that add or subtract value to the offering and can be grouped into four categories: brand loyalty, brand awareness, perceived quality and brand associations.

Characterizing the brand as an asset – or a liability – made it strategic rather than tactical and thus had significant organizational and resource implications. Explicitly conceptualizing brand loyalty as part of brand equity rather than its outcome was important as it then elevated customer loyalty to the status of a brand asset. The book also provided a rationale for building brands by explaining exactly how a strong brand added value, a rationale that is needed by marketing executives attempting to change their role within the firm to be strategic as well as tactical.

You followed that with three more books: *Building Strong Brands* in 1996, *Brand Leadership* in 2000 and *Brand Portfolio Strategy* in 2004. Were you pleased with their reception?

I was. It seemed I had caught a wave that has persisted. And even more significantly for me, I was influencing operating executives, which was a first for me. I was frankly stunned by the impact that the books have on managerial audiences. It turns out that executives read books and adopt ideas they are attracted to. The influence of the books made me realize how invisible my previous work had been in terms of the 'real world'.

Building Strong Brands, which was designed to help firms actually manage their brands, was particularly impactful. Published in 1996, it introduced my 'brand identity' model of brand management which is used in many organizations as the basis for their strategic brand management. The basic philosophy was that a brand is more than a single claim. In fact, it needs to have from six to 12 dimensions; they should include more than attribute dimensions, and they need to be prioritized.

The other two books built on that foundation. *Brand Leadership* (with Erich Joachimsthaler) expanded the brand identity model, introduced some ideas around going beyond advertising to build brands, and reported on a global brand management study. *Brand Portfolio Strategy*, for the first time, brought concepts and ideas together to address the messy problem of creating and managing a portfolio of brands.

So your seminal work on brands was not part of a grand plan?

My interest in brands and the subsequent research, articles and books was actually a bit of happenstance. In fact, during the first 15 years or more of my academic career, I was all over the map and very undisciplined. My own brand was very confused and badly managed. I was supposed to be a quantitative modeller but I got interested in consumer protection, emotions in advertising, psychology and strategy, and wrote books on advertising, marketing research and strategy. There was no vision or pattern.

However, looking back, this variety of interests was pivotal in my ability to contribute to the branding area. My branding effort, particularly my early research and my first brand book, drew heavily on much of my earlier writings and research both in substance and in skills developed. I could never have gotten started without that background.

Charlie Draper, a legend at the Massachusetts Institute of Technology, was an eternal student, getting a degree in almost every undergraduate discipline before he finally got a PhD. This academic dilettante discovered inertial navigation and became one of the greatest aeronautical engineering innovators of all time. One reason for his success was that he 'wasted' much of his time taking all these courses instead of figuring out what he wanted to do. His parents probably wondered if he was ever going to get out of undergraduate school. I am no Charlie Draper, for sure, but I do share with him the experience of being able to draw on a broad array of fields and skills in order to contribute to a worthwhile area.

How did your relationship with Prophet occur?

During the 1990s I gradually did more and more consulting which I found stimulating and rewarding. In 1998, I decided to join Prophet, then a San Francisco marketing consulting company with 16 people started by a former student, in order to leverage my time and ideas. Since then the firm has grown to 100 people with offices in Chicago, New York, Europe and Japan and its offerings, which at one time were based around my books, have expanded into related areas.

So you now combine both consulting and your research work?

My consulting time is highly leveraged. I meet with consulting teams often by phone, sometimes attend key client meetings, and contribute to the firm's intellectual capability and marketing effort. Much of my effort is directed towards giving talks and conducting research, plus writing books and articles. My research tends to be practical, like my latest study on chief marketing officers (CMOs) and how they manage across silos.

Why did you choose to spend so much more of your time away from academia?

I wanted to make an impact on business management. In particular, I had two goals. The first was to communicate the importance of building assets, especially brand assets, and reducing the relative influence of short-term financials on managers' behaviour. The second was to create concepts and methods to help firms build and manage brands and brand portfolios. I felt I could do this best outside of the academic environment and did not feel it was fair to the Haas School to engage so extensively in non-academic activities as a full-time professor.

There was another factor. I was stimulated by the real problems of real companies and increasingly found academic research to be less and less interesting. Academic research in the research business schools such as London Business School, INSEAD, Wharton, Northwestern, Stanford or Berkeley tends to be highly abstract. The focus is on creating theories and applying concepts and methods from economics, statistics, psychology, sociology and other respected academic disciplines to test those theories. The goal is to publish respected articles and gain peer recognition for doing rigorous work.

These articles are usually intellectually impressive and persuasive. However, they rarely have much relevance to real world issues that are facing executives. They either deal with highly artificial environments or with rather trivial issues. In either case, they are not easily transferred to the real world. Of course, I played in that world for over two decades.

I should hasten to say that being a professor is extremely stimulating and enjoyable. The colleagues are bright and creative. You have freedom to do whatever interests you (after you make tenure at least) when and where you want to do it. However, I advise those who aspire to be a professor to read academic journals to make sure that such research will interest them.

Accepted wisdom says that academic research can be irrelevant to business. What is your opinion?

I am certainly not the only academic attempting to influence managers. There are at least several dozen professors whose research and writing are motivated by important business problems and many more for whom some of their research would be considered helpful to managers. They tend to be established professors with tenure because it is hard to mix practical research with the type of academic articles that will lead to tenure.

This group, which tends to write books, a commodity not generally helpful to an academic reputation, would include people such as George Day, Ted Levitt, Len Berry, Phil Kotler, Jerry Tellis, Jerry Wind, Pat Barwise, John Quelch, Jean-Claude Larreche, Glen Urban and there are more. However, their output still represents a small percentage of the research and writing in academic marketing.

Your name has become synonymous with branding. What is your feeling about that?

I am always surprised, to say the least, when I hear that. It does seem true that the brand equity movement has, if anything, continued to grow over the last decade and that is very rewarding although I had a lot of help in making that happen.

When I hear about my specific models being used, I am usually stunned. I was in Japan recently, and three people, one from a political party, came up to me at an event to say that their organization is using my brand identity model. Such an event is not uncommon and I am always pleased. However, on closer examination, it sometimes turns out that their application of the model is faulty. That is in part due to the fact that the model was not refined and elaborated in *Building Strong Brands* and many never got exposed to the *Brand Leadership* book, which did so.

What challenges have you faced along the way?

Executives are often hard to get on board because they are preoccupied with other issues such as downsizing, outsourcing, addressing quality problems, etc. and have a lot of pressure to deliver short-term profits. A study concluded that under 24% of 350 chief executive officers (CEOs) see marketing as an important business discipline.

A related challenge is to demonstrate the value of brand building. There is an enormous pressure for accountability, to show that brand-building investments achieve an acceptable return on investment (ROI). Like any intangible asset such as people and IT, where the pay-off is far in the future, it's difficult to prove ROI results except for short-term tactical programs.

What is the best way to get CEOs on board?

Manage the context by talking in terms of the CEO's priority agenda. Focus on growth objectives instead of brand extensions, efficiency and cost objectives instead of marketing synergy or scale, and building assets to support strategic initiatives instead of brand image campaigns. Another approach is to demonstrate value by quantifying success stories, perhaps based on market tests.

Finally, who have been the main figures that have influenced your work?

In no particular order, Peter Drucker showed me – particularly through his book *Managing for Results* – how to get beyond short-term financials to manage an enterprise. Ted Levitt, meanwhile, explained in graphic detail that an offering is more than its attributes. People want holes, not drill bits. My co-authors – especially Bob Jacobson and Kevin Keller – provided substance and ideas. My daughter Jennifer pushed me to be rigorous.

Current views of marketing

What is your current view of marketing? How has it changed in the intervening years, and why?

There is a tension in most firms with respect to marketing. Should it be strategic or tactical? Should it be centralized or decentralized? There are efforts to change marketing to make it more strategic and centralized, but the pace is spotty. Another major change is that mass communication vehicles that marketers have relied on in the past are much less effective and dominant, so there is a need to develop and manage new brand-building efforts.

Where do you think it's going wrong? Going right?

I think it varies by firm. Those firms that are blessed with a depth of marketing talent and an externally oriented CEO with marketing instincts, such as Procter & Gamble (P&G), are making good progress. But those firms that lack a marketing capability and have technical or finance-oriented CEOs often flounder. They frequently encounter situations where marketing, and especially branding, is undeniably important but they don't have a clue what to do.

There is often a tipping point, a point at which the CEO who was a spectator becomes engaged. That often occurs when there is a new business strategy that is not supported adequately by the current brand assets. Brand strategy, as a result, becomes a priority and the CEO gets involved in making it happen. Sometimes the CEO, who was recently on the sidelines, then becomes an evangelist for brands.

There is a tension in most firms with respect to marketing. Should it be strategic or tactical? Should it be centralized or decentralized? There are efforts to change marketing to make it more strategic and centralized, but the pace is spotty.

What happens when they reach that tipping point?

The CEO often gets personally involved in articulating the business strategy, creating a vision for the brand, linking the vision to the values and culture of the organization, and helping to communicate that vision. They usually also actively attempt to find a CMO and marketing team that are competent and credible using internal or external sources or both. Until that tipping point is reached, it's hard to get on their radar screen. They view marketing as tactical. It's something that can be delegated, that they needn't worry about.

You do a lot of work in Japan, don't you?

Yes, since 1975 I have made over 25 trips to Japan and given nearly 100 talks there. I used to go there once every other year but since 2001 when I became an advisor to Denstu (the largest advertising agency in the world), I now go three times a year.

What's the difference between Japanese and American companies?

Four differences have been salient in my work. First, in Japan the organization still respects rank and age (which often inhibits the upgrading of the marketing talent, which is generally weaker than in the USA), very different from the emerging flat entrepreneurial organizations of the States. Second, while there is an eagerness for getting ideas through speakers and training, there is a reluctance to use consultants.

Third, there is a tendency to build decision models that are very complex and complete while in the USA the decision-making tends to be more focused. Finally, I have much more access to CEOs in Japan than I do in the USA, in part because academics are more respected in Japan and in part because the Japanese CEO is less of a hands-on manager in Japan and thus has time to see people like me.

Do you find that they actually put into practice what you're saying to them better than elsewhere?

I think they absorb what I am saying. Unlike my US audiences the Japanese managers are attentive and take notes. I see my ideas being applied frequently. However, I also see the initiatives being inhibited or stymied by the organizational hierarchy. Of course, it depends on the firm. Those few firms, such as Shisheido and Sony, which have more of a marketing orientation and talent, find it easier to accept new ideas and develop effective new programs.

In the USA the role of the CMO seems to be becoming more prevalent. Is this helping to raise the stature of marketers?

Without question. There is a new breed of CMO coming along with two major goals. The first is to get control of product and/or geographic silos, which are prevalent in virtually all organizations, from General Motors (GM) to Hewlett Packard to Unilever to Citigroup. Each silo has its own marketing group that has an 'I know this market and you don't' orientation. Unfettered decentralization has a host of advantages including fostering business vitality and adaptability but also results in unacceptable inefficiencies and lost opportunities. As a result firms are realizing that accountability and central control of brands and programs need to be introduced.

The second is to provide market driven growth to the firm. In many cases the firm, which may have relied on downsizing and acquisitions to achieve financial performance, has explicitly targeted the need to grow internally. The CMO naturally needs to own this effort if it is to be more than ad hoc initiatives.

The challenge is how to introduce a CMO-led central marketing to resistant organizations.

Why are some organizations resistant to this new breed of CMO?

The decentralized units are reluctant to lose power and budget to a central group for selfish reasons and also because they believe they simply know better. They can access political and process tools to obstruct a new CMO. Further, it is often easy to relegate marketing to a tactical role and resist including the CMO as a driving partner for a strategic growth strategy. So it can be difficult for a new CMO to achieve credibility and effectiveness in a resistant organization. One study said that the average life of a CMO is 18 or 20 months, which is a dramatic commentary on the job.

What advice would you give to these CMOs about managing brands across product and geographic silos?

I recently completed a CMO study that provided some guidelines. First, attempt to get the CEO on board and leverage that involvement. Second, create a strong team that can demonstrate competence and results. Third, develop and use cross-business task forces and teams to break down silos. Fourth, get easy wins to demonstrate success. Fifth, play the facilitator role, which is much less threatening than more ambitious roles, to influence strategy. Sixth, deliver excellence, starting with the brand vision. Excellence attracts supporters. Finally, don't over-centralize but balance central opportunities and local needs.

In general, what would you say are the top challenges that marketers face?

There are a host of challenges. Within the brand arena, in particular, I would say that relevance and differentiation are two of the most difficult and serious challenges.

Understanding relevance is the key to strategy in dynamic markets and today all firms operate in dynamic markets. Emerging product categories and subcategories change the competitive landscape. Some firms are driving those changes and have an opportunity to become leaders in a new market or submarket, shaping what customers are buying. Those that are successful – such as Toyota with its Prius, Cirque Du Soleil, CNN, Apple with the iPod, Starbucks, and Vanguard with index funds – have enjoyed exceptional market and financial success, lasting years.

Other firms need to make sure that they do not become less relevant as competitors develop new categories and subcategories. It is possible to make the greatest sports utility vehicle (SUV) in the world with the most loyal customers and an envied image. However, if a significant number of your customers now want a hybrid, it simply does not matter how good your SUV is perceived to be; you are less relevant than before and will see your sales eroding. These firms need to detect trends that will change the marketplace, evaluate those trends, develop responsive products or services, and have a brand portfolio strategy in place that provides a credible brand, sub-brand or endorsed brand that will carry the flag. Not easy.

How can companies stay ahead of the game in terms of relevance?

Innovation is the key. One type, disruptive innovation, will create new categories or subcategories. Such innovation can involve technology but often can also be based on a different business model. Enterprise-Rent-Car, for example, came from obscurity to become the sales and profit leader by focusing on the needs of insurance companies to provide drivers with rental cars when their cars were being repaired. Another type, sustaining innovation, can help avoid being surpassed by competitors and can also help a firm leapfrog a competitor's advance.

What makes a successful innovator?

Being successful at innovation involves more than a research and development budget. The organizations, people, processes and culture have to be supportive of innovation. It also involves having a brand portfolio and strategy that enable the firm to own and leverage the innovation. Too many innovations are lost because they are not branded or the brands are not managed over time. Finally, it involves really understanding the customer and customer trends. Ethnographic research has helped firms like P&G and others to innovate.

What about your second challenge, differentiation?

Most brands are facing overcapacity, vigorous price pressures and margin erosion because, in part, product differentiation is hard to maintain in the face of advances that are copied so swiftly. Product class after product class is maturing, becoming boring and lifeless. The challenge is to create and maintain energy and points of differentiation.

One suggestion is, when developing a brand identity and position, to augment or replace product attributes and customer benefits with brand personality and/or organization associations – they're easier to differentiate than products. A personality can not only make a brand stand out but make it more approachable and/or credible as well. While product attributes are easily duplicated, an organization's culture, values and programs will often be unique.

Another is to introduce branded differentiators, actively managed branded features, ingredients, services or programs that create a meaningful, impactful point of differentiation over an extended period. Westin Hotels' 'Heavenly Bed', GM's Onstar system, Tide's Stain Detective, UPS's Supply Chain Solutions, Cadillac's Northstar engine and Amazon's One-Click have all provided a lasting point of differentiation.

How big an impact has evolving technology had on your current view of marketing?

It has had a huge impact on how you go about brand building. Mass media advertising is becoming much less important because of its fragmentation and the growth of alternative sources of information and entertainment, most of which is driven by technology.

Are there any myths about marketing you would like to see dispelled?

That marketing is advertising or, more generally communication, and is tactical, and can be delegated to communication staff.

How can people identify fads as opposed to important new techniques?

That is the key question as far as relevance is concerned. Peter Drucker once said that fads are things people talk about and trends are what they actually do. The key is to understand the customer and what they value. A 'trend' to one-stop financial shopping in the early 1980s died because customers did not value it.

Companies are increasingly saying: we're going to wrap our product into a service because otherwise we'll just become a commodity. Do you have a view on whether this is a fad or an actual trend?

In some contexts adding services to augment the product, moving from selling components to offering systems solutions, will provide a differentiating added value. The question is: how many customers really care enough to pay for it? That's always the hard issue. Sometimes there are just too few of them to make it worthwhile.

What do you think that marketers need to be excellent at to prosper in the modern environment?

Increasingly, marketers need to understand brand portfolio management and its role in managing change and dealing with the relevance issue. Firms are discovering that their brand portfolio is a mess, confusing, inefficient and incapable of dealing with the dynamics of the business.

Organizational skills will also become more important – firms are looking for people who are naturally collaborative as they deal with silo issues. It's almost back to the days of the original brand managers – a lot of responsibility and little authority.

I also believe that the creativity of both individuals and organizations will be something that differentiates the successful firm of the future from the also-rans. There is an increasing premium on the home-run marketing programs and the new business model that creates a new category or sub-category.

Getting more personal

What impact, if any, did your early environment and upbringing have on your career?

If I look at my grandparents, they were hard workers too, but in different fields. One grandfather was a lawyer, the other a farmer, then a merchant and finally a postmaster. They were both very conscientious about what they did and anecdotes suggest they always worked hard and tried to do as good a job as they could. My father, an engineering manager for AT&T, was in the same mould. Of course, they all lived in such different eras that it's a little bit hard to compare. But I think there is that common thread – a Norwegian background that produces people who are conscientious and work hard.

> *Writing my autobiography,* From Fargo to the World of Brands, *caused me to reflect on the fact that I've always been motivated to practise and learn, whether at tennis, golf or whatever, and to work long hours to do the best I could.*

I think I picked up some of that work ethic plus a desire to excel within the limits of my talents. Writing my autobiography, *From Fargo to the World of Brands*, caused me to reflect on the fact that I've always been motivated to practise and learn, whether at tennis, golf or whatever, and to work long hours to do the best I could. Curiously, I think my daughter is in the same mould. Jennifer, now a Stanford professor, is an extremely successful academic, working in the areas of cultural impact on consumer behaviour, consumer emotions, and the psychology of brand relationships.

What's the main thing you've taken from living and working in Japan?

I just love being in Japan – the lights, the energy, the politeness, the commitment of the taxicab drivers and doormen, the Sumo tournaments, the ryokans (traditional Japanese inns), Japanese friends, the flowers in the restaurants, Mt Fuji, the female caddies controlling four golf bags, the trains, tatami mats, the food, uniformed schoolchildren, the formalities, cherry blossoms, sushi, and the Ginza (the most exclusive and expensive shopping area in Japan) are all special.

It's a hard question, but is there any one part of your life that you're particularly proud of?

My autobiography, *From Fargo to the World of Brands*, goes into detail. Personally, I am very proud of our family, my three daughters, and my relationship with my close friends. My three daughters in particular are wonderful people, successful professionals, and have their own impressive families. I am very lucky to have seen them develop and to continue to be a daily part of their lives.

Professionally I am most proud of my work on branding and my efforts, however modest, to influence the thinking and actions of managers and firms. My four books, especially *Building Strong Brands*, have had an influence that has been rewarding. I am also proud of my work in Japan where I have probably had more influence than in the USA.

Selected publications

Books

Strategic Market Management, John Wiley & Sons, Inc. 2007, eighth edition.
From Fargo to the World of Brands: My Story So Far, Iceni Books, 2005.

Brand Portfolio Strategy: Creating Relevance, Differentiation, Energy, Leverage and Clarity, The Free Press, 2004.

Marketing Research, John Wiley & Sons, Inc. Co-author: George S. Day and since the fifth edition by V. Kumer. 8th edn published in 2004.

Brand Leadership, The Free Press, 2000. Co-author: Erich Joachimsthaler.

Building Strong Brands, The Free Press, 1996.

Advertising Management, Prentice-Hall, 1996, 5th edn. Co-author: John G. Myers and since the fourth edition Rajeev Batra. Also translated into Japanese and Spanish.

Managing Brand Equity, The Free Press, 1991.

Consumerism: Search for the Consumer Interest, The Free Press, 1982, 4th edn. Co-editor: George S. Day.

Multivariate Analysis in Marketing: Theory and Applications (editor), Wadsworth Publishing Company, 1971. 2nd edn published by The Scientific Press, 1981.

Articles

'The Relevance of Relevance: Innovating Brands in Fast-Moving Markets', *Strategy + Business*, Spring, 2004. Introduces and illustrates brand relevance.

'The Power of a Branded Differentiator', *Sloan Management Review*, Fall, 2003, pp. 83–92. Introduced the concept of brand differentiator.

'The Value Relevance of Brand Attitude in High Technology Markets', *Journal of Marketing Research* (with Bob Jacobson), November, 2001, pp. 485–493. Showed that in the high tech sector, brand equity as measured by attitude pays off.

'The Lure of Global Branding' (with Erich Joachimsthaler), *Harvard Business Review*, November–December, 1999. Reported on a study of how firms manage their brand globally.

'Should You Take Your Brand to Where the Action Is?', *Harvard Business Review*, October–November, 1997, pp. 135–143. Discussed vertical brand extensions.

'Brand Building in the "Post-Media" Age: Lessons from Europe' (with Erich Joachimsthaler), *Harvard Business Review*, January–February, 1997, pp. 39–50. Used examples from Europe to show how to go beyond advertising to build brands.

'The Saturn Story: Building a Brand', *California Management Review*, Winter, 1994. The best article award winner, told a dramatic brand-building story.

'Consumer Evaluations of Brand Extensions' (with Kevin Lane Keller), *Journal of Marketing*, 1990, Vol. 54, pp. 27–41.

'The Strategic Role of Product Quality' (with Robert Jacobson), *Journal of Marketing*, October, 1987, pp. 31–44. The best article award winner, showed how brand equity as measured by perceived quality pays off in terms of market share and profitability.

'The Perils of High Growth Markets' (with George S. Day), *Strategic Management Journal*, 7, September–October, 1986, pp. 409–421. Argued that high growth markets are risky.

'Warmth in Advertising: Measurement, Impact and Sequence Effects' (with Douglas Stayman and Michael R. Hagerty), *Journal of Consumer Research*, March, 1986, pp. 1–15. One of the most cited *JCR* articles, it defined warmth and demonstrated its impact.

'Is Market Share All that It's Cracked Up to Be?' (with Robert Jacobson), *Journal of Marketing*, Fall, 1985, pp. 11–22. Showed that investing to build share will improve profitability much less than had been assumed.

3

Jean-Claude Larreche

Marketing strategy master

Professor Jean-Claude Larreche is the holder of the Alfred H. Heineken Chair at INSEAD. He is a specialist in strategic marketing and directs a number of activities aimed at achieving excellence in customer centricity. These include corporate assessments, measurement tools, the 'Customer Focus: From Promise to Action' executive program which he has created at INSEAD, and a forthcoming book.

From 1998 to 2002, Larreche authored five annual reports on Measuring the Competitive Fitness of Global Firms *(Financial Times Prentice Hall) presenting the assessment of leading global firms on capabilities such as customer orientation, innovation, marketing operations, e-business and human resources.*

He is also chairman of StratX SA, a company specializing in strategic marketing training and services. He was a member of the INSEAD Board for 14 years and a member of the board of Reckitt Benckiser plc from 1983 to 2001. He is the founder of several INSEAD executive programs, including 'Customer Focus: From Promise to Action', 'Strategic Management of Services', and 'Advanced Industrial Marketing'. He is a consultant to several multinational corporations and has taught in many executive development courses.

Larreche's publications have appeared in numerous international journals. He is the author and co-author of several books, including: Marketing Management: A Strategic Decision-Making Approach *and* Marketing Strategy: Planning and Implementation *(with Orville Walker, Harper Boyd and John Mullins),* Markstrat *(with Hubert Gatignon), and* Industrat *(with David Weinstein). He has also received a number of professional awards and honours.*

He received a PhD in business from Stanford University and an MBA from INSEAD. Before his business studies, he qualified as an electronics engineer from INSA (Lyon) and obtained an MSc in computer sciences from the University of London.

The professional journey

What would you say you are best known for?

I would say that I am best known for marketing excellence and customer focus.

Marketing excellence deals with marketing people. It's about making them better at marketing professionalism and leadership. And I would define marketing professionalism as ensuring that marketers are systematic about their approaches – not leaving things halfway through, but making decisions based on all the relevant facts.

Marketing leadership, meanwhile, means that marketing should spearhead the company in its markets and take it forward, keeping it ahead of competition. I believe that marketing should therefore combine the fundamentals of marketing professionalism and market leadership.

My other specialism is customer focus, where the whole company should be focused on customers. It involves cultural changes affecting not just marketers, but the company in its entirety. It means signing up people from research and development, manufacturing, human resources, finance and from all around the world to a program that will make the whole company more customer-focused.

How did your career start?

My background was very scientific. My first degree was in electronic engineering. Then I did an MSc in computer sciences in London, because the French at the time were not advanced enough in that area. I recall that I used to know 14 computer languages. When I was 23, I wrote the first book in French about the Basic programming language.

When was this?

This was in 1970. But when I sent the manuscript to the publisher he said the book wouldn't work because nobody would know what I was talking about. I said, 'But that's exactly why I wrote it!' Then I did my MBA at INSEAD, a PhD in marketing at Stanford University and, on my return, combined all that with my interests and background in computers. I had an interest in areas such as artificial intelligence and robotics, which was quite ahead of the time but focused, of course, on marketing.

What was the trigger for you to go into marketing?

I'd just finished my MBA at INSEAD, when I got a phone call from L'Oréal. The company had been approached by a consulting firm trying to sell it the first marketing model, from the Massachusetts Institute of Technology

(MIT), and wanted someone from INSEAD who knew something about it.

The problem was that marketing models were so new nobody was even teaching the subject there. And I was just a research assistant. So the then-dean, Dean Berry (his first name was also Dean), said to me, 'You are the only one who can help because of your background in computers, plus you have an MBA from INSEAD and you're already researching with us.'

At the time, though, my research was in computers and operations research. Even so, I went and saw L'Oréal, trying to help it understand the model the consulting company was trying to sell. I ended up consulting for L'Oréal on the launch of a new product, using this model called Sprinter, developed by Glen Urban, an MIT professor.

So this, then, was seminal?

Yes. For me as a young kid, aged 24, who'd just got my MBA and was a research assistant at INSEAD, it was fantastic. So then I decided to investigate the best places in the world to study marketing modelling. Harvard, MIT and Stanford were top of the list, so I applied and was admitted to all three. I then asked around for advice and was told, don't go to Harvard because it's not research-oriented enough, which was probably true at the time. So that meant choosing between MIT and Stanford. Since California was where things happened, I picked Stanford and stayed there from 1971 to 1974.

I had wanted to study there under Dave Montgomery, who was known as the best PhD adviser on the subject of marketing modelling. But Dave, who'd just written the first book on the subject with Glen Urban, wanted to take on only one PhD student at a time. Fortunately he liked me and also had a very good opinion about Europeans generally (who were supposed to be better at mathematics than his American students). So I was very privileged to have Dave as a PhD adviser. It was a fantastic time and we've remained friends ever since.

What attracted you to this field? Was it the fact that you were being given the chance to nail a rather esoteric concept?

Well, I was there at the beginning of marketing modelling, but I didn't invent it. Dave Montgomery, Glen Urban, people like Bill Massy, John

Little, Robert Buzzell, Frank Bass – around half a dozen of them – had, in the previous five to eight years, created this whole field.

So what did you think you could bring to the party, and what was the challenge?

Nothing, really. I was just excited by the subject and motivated by my own selfish pleasure. That's what happens when you're 24 and know nothing about the world of business! By the time I returned to INSEAD from Stanford, however, I was very research-oriented, which I hadn't been before I went to the USA.

Let me give you a bit of background. Until 1974, professors at INSEAD came from business and usually lacked PhDs. So Dean Berry, who had joined INSEAD in 1972, wanted to build up its academic reputation. When I returned from California, we were a small group of people, all with very new US PhDs in fields such as finance and so on. It amounted to a youth revolution. The oldest professor at INSEAD was not yet 40 years old. We were, in fact, the first European academic professors to be recognized by the American business school community.

It was then that I decided on my research goal: I wanted to develop *the* mega marketing model. It would combine everything that was known about marketing modelling because, at the time, they were either total monsters – simulating the customer, at the individual level – or they were specialized, like an advertising model here, a pricing model there, a distribution model here and a sales force model there. I wanted my model to integrate that with some of the most recent things about positioning, segmentation, multidimensional scaling and all that.

I recruited an assistant, Hubert Gatignon, to work with me in this project. But then I received a memo from the head of the centre which was funding this, asking why I was using the budget for research and not teaching. He said that this was unacceptable, that the budget was meant to be used to write case studies to help teaching. To my mind, research does help teaching, and it doesn't have to be in a direct way.

What did you do?

I didn't like the idea of writing case studies at the time. And besides, I was in modelling up to my neck. It was a passion. So I had to think fast and that's why I repositioned my research model as a teaching simulation. It became Markstrat, which stands for marketing strategy.

It took three years to develop and the results were published in 1977. And, although my interest was not in developing teaching materials but in pure research, it was good that I did it, because my research project was so ambitious that it couldn't have been developed without having access to a dozen or so programmers.

Then I visited an American friend, Ed Strong, who was on sabbatical at the business school IMEDE (which went on to become IMD) in Lausanne. IMEDE had been created (and part-funded) by Nestlé in the late 1970s. I'd brought along a draft of the Markstrat manual to see what he thought.

On my return to INSEAD, I got a phone call from someone who asked whether I was Jean Claude Larreche and had I developed something called Markstrat. I replied, 'Yes', but asked, 'How have you come across it because it hasn't even been published yet?'

He said, 'I'm from Nestlé. I've read it and it's exactly what we need to train our product managers because it will help them become much more strategic. Currently, they're much too short-term-focused.'

I was delighted. In 1976 I was a young 28-year-old professor, not yet doing any consulting apart from what I'd done for L'Oréal. Nestlé adopted Markstrat, and used it for the next 20 years. Hubert Gatignon, my assistant and co-author, later obtained a PhD at UCLA, joined the Wharton Faculty, and came back to INSEAD where he eventually became dean of faculty.

Did interest in it grow?

The second call came in 1978 from the New York headquarters of General Electric (GE) once Markstrat had been published in book form. GE said, 'We've looked at it and it's fantastic. Can we talk about it?' I think it still uses a version today, some 30 years on.

So at a very young age, through the Markstrat simulation, I got into 'culture change'. Nestlé may have been about educating its product managers, but GE was much more about transforming its culture to be more customer-focused. And then over the next 30 years, many other companies used Markstrat to develop their people towards one of these two goals:

marketing excellence and customer-based culture. The perceived impact was so good that several of my clients led Markstrat-based initiatives in every job they moved to.

I was very lucky. It was a fantastic experience, and revolved around something that was relatively minor in my portfolio of activities. Markstrat never made my academic reputation. Articles in the *Journal of Marketing Research*, the *Journal of Marketing Science* and so on were what made my name in the field. I started as assistant professor, then associate professor, then became full professor, and finally I received the Alfred H. Heineken chair.

What did Markstrat offer companies when it first emerged?

It enabled segmentation and positioning, and encompassed all areas of the marketing mix at a time when, remember, marketing consisted of the 4Ps. But more importantly, it provided a realistic simulated environment where managers could learn, test their understanding, develop new attitudes and act differently when back in their jobs. In that way it was truly innovative. It is now distributed and continually enhanced by my firm StratX and the online version was launched in 2005. Thirty years after its first publication, Markstrat is used actively by about 500 business schools worldwide, including 24 of the top 30 US schools.

It's an approach that keeps evolving and improving all the time. It's rather like trying to define marketing: it's not a product, it's a concept. People have talked about the death of the product manager for some 20 years, but they're still around. They may become extinct one day, but marketing won't die. And Markstrat will exist as long as we keep investing in it.

What made you decide to set up your own company?

When I started, I was immersed in academic research and a whole sequence of events made me realize that this meant I wasn't influencing much except other academics. It may have been fantastic in terms of research, but it was never used by a business corporation.

So after a few years, I developed an interest in helping to change companies. I became more involved in working with companies, and eventually created, StratX. It, of course, has developed a multitude of simulations, covering different marketing situations in different industries. I eventually stopped publishing in academic journals and concentrated more on business-oriented publications. I have written two books with American colleagues: one on marketing management, the other one on marketing strategy. In addition I have always had some research going on, like the competitive fitness reports, *Measuring the Competitive Fitness of Global Firms*.

If you teach philosophy, maths or physics you transmit knowledge, but in business we should be very different. We should go beyond knowledge; we should change attitudes, and help people do better. In that context, we're much closer to a school of medicine or law, in my view, than to a school of science. And that's what led to the development of StratX 20 years ago: to bridge that gap between the transmission of knowledge and action leading to impact.

StratX has had a lot of influence on many major companies. For instance, out of the top 10 pharmaceutical companies worldwide, we have five of them as clients. In the USA, meanwhile, we still have General Electric as a client, along with Boeing and Pfizer. In Europe, we have Novartis, L'Oréal, Philip Morris International and many other big companies.

If you teach philosophy, maths or physics you transmit knowledge, but in business we should be very different. We should go beyond knowledge; we should change attitudes, and help people do better. In that context, we're much closer to a school of medicine or law, in my view, than to a school of science.

Even though we're small – some 50 people – we influence organizations that are much larger.

How did you decide, with StratX, on the right balance between the theoretical and the practical?

StratX has been growing reasonably over time, but it could have grown even bigger if we'd wanted to go into consulting at full speed. Instead, we pursued the 'high ground' strategy, and see ourselves as positioned between business schools and consulting companies. We don't want to compete with consulting companies – that's a different ball game. So that's why we try to offer a combination of theory and practice. We work with business schools all the time.

How would you categorize your life to date?

My adult life as an academic has, to date, consisted of three phases. The first has been in academic research and, by accident, getting into influencing business. The second has involved helping business corporations from both inside and outside INSEAD. The third, which I started in 2005, is putting all that down in writing so that it can influence more people than just my direct customers. And that's why now I have several books in preparation and why life never stops going at full speed.

Now you're in your third phase, are you still teaching, when you're not writing?

Sure, I've been teaching all the time. I love it.

What does it give to you? Does it keep the ideas coming?

That, plus it's a good way of testing things. For my next book to be published in 2007, for instance, I have tested so many things in the last two years of which I thought I was 100% sure. I try to test variations. My colleagues are amazed that, given my experience, I keep changing what I'm teaching – not so much the overall subject, but the content.

Well, presumably it's one way of keeping boredom at bay?

Exactly. I don't know how some others can teach the same thing, day in, day out, while they don't understand why I keep changing something that works very well already.

Current views on marketing

What's your feeling about marketing currently?

I now split the marketers I meet between those who will remain in marketing forever and those who have chief executive officer (CEO) potential. These are two different categories. It's not that one is better than the other, but it's a choice.

There's a third category, of course: the people who will have to drop out of marketing because they didn't make it. Those who are most interesting, and who I try to develop further, are the ones who eventually will be CEO material. That's my ambition as a consultant and academic. Some people will tell me, 'I don't want to be a CEO' and that's fair enough. But if they stay in marketing they should have a CEO-like mind. That's what I'm talking about when I refer to marketing professionalism and marketing leadership.

So where is marketing going right?

I think it's when we talk about things like the return on investment (ROI) of marketing. Because of pressure from the shareholders, marketing is ultimately becoming more conscious of effectiveness and efficiency.

Unfortunately, there's still a huge gap between some of the writing of my colleagues in academia, when they talk about marketing ROI, and my conversations with CEOs on the same topic. In academic circles, marketing ROI refers to very specific marketing tactics, such as promotions, advertising or selling.

The CEOs' take on marketing ROI, however, is talking about marketing in general and whether there is a good return on the money invested into the department. These are two separate definitions of ROI.

You remember the old adage, right? 'I know half of my advertising budget is being wasted, but I don't know which half'? Well, it's still true to a large extent, but now there are so many forces at play including competition and shareholders, that those marketers who do waste money won't have a great future any more.

Unfortunately, many marketing people are much more attracted by fashion than they are by professionalism. And too many of these fashion victims of marketing are looking for two things: 'What's new?' and 'How can I get a bigger budget?'. If you go to marketing departments you'll see how very often they're very far from professional.

> *Unfortunately, many marketing people are much more attracted by fashion than they are by professionalism. And too many of these fashion victims of marketing are looking for two things: 'What's new?' and 'How can I get a bigger budget?'. If you go to marketing departments you'll see how very often they're very far from professional.*

What advice would you give to those marketers who want to get ahead?

Well, frankly some of these people still end up getting promoted. How so? Because they're lucky. If you ride a good wave in marketing, you can have good results for the wrong reasons. It might happen once, twice, maybe three times, but eventually it will catch up with you.

Even if you're very successful or very lucky, you still may stop at some level. There are a lot of good chief marketing officers (CMOs), full of enthusiasm, newness and big budgets who never make it to CEO level. They've had to resign, and most of them are on the conference circuit, writing books about branding or other hot topics.

It's unfortunate because good companies have probably lost some very competent marketing people, who were not able to develop themselves as general managers. If these people had the stamina to become CEOs then we would have in all of these companies great CEOs who also used to be CMOs.

What is holding them back, in your view?

It is generally a deficiency in one or more of three areas: business acumen, leadership of people and the ability to inspire trust.

Isn't it sometimes the company structure that militates against marketers moving up the corporate ladder?

No, no, no. Frankly I've met a lot of them. You see them jumping up and down with their latest magic formulas provided by advertising agencies or other suppliers, failing to listen or to ponder advantages and drawbacks – all the basic stuff that is at the heart of being a CEO. They come up with punchlines all the time, while you can see the CEOs getting their measure in the first four or five minutes.

After two years of consultancy work for Reckitt & Colman (now Reckitt Benckiser) in London – I had been brought in by Dave Montgomery, who was working for the company in Australia – the CEO asked if I'd join the main board. I was 36, 20 years younger than the youngest board member. I was also the only foreigner and the only academic. I stayed on that board for 18 years.

The CEO at the time, John West, was famous for his ability to judge people swiftly. He was a great leader and we had a spirited discussion one day about how quickly he judged people. Here I was, 36 years old, telling this guy who was 60 years old that you cannot judge someone in five minutes. Still, he debated with me and justified it by saying that when you've got 30 years of experience as he had, you have to make quick decisions and decide very fast if a person is good or not for a job. He was right.

He would know, by their behaviour, looking at their eyes or by listening to them. He wasn't even judging CVs. Since then, I've learnt that this is what sets the good CEOs apart from the poor ones: the ability to evaluate people very fast and be right in that evaluation. So now, maybe, I have fallen into that trap of looking at marketing people systematically and asking myself every time I see them: 'Are they CEO material?' And, having done it for 20 years, you end up being good at it.

Are there any case studies you'd like to put forward to illustrate how a company or organization can get it right – or wrong?

There are some obvious examples. One must never forget companies who got it wrong, like IBM in the 1980s. It ended up losing $8 bn in 1993 as a result of poor marketing. Yet it was the best marketing company in business-to-business. Likewise, Procter & Gamble (P&G), the best marketing company in business-to-consumers, got it wrong in the late 1990s. Its chairman/CEO was fired by the board. Yet, now, A.G. Lafley has led a fantastic P&G comeback in the last five years. So even the best can get it totally wrong, but can also find the ability to come back under the proper leadership.

There are others who've been doing it wrong for a long time, are continuing to do so, and it will take a miracle for them to change. This includes the American automobile companies, some of the oil companies and most retail banks. They are protected from full competition by networks, oil shortages or high customer switching costs, but will be vulnerable in the longer term.

Given the profits that the oil companies are posting, is this really true?

Look at the background to the profits. The number one determinant of their profitability is the price of oil. It's been like that for the last 30 years, ever since the first oil crisis. It has nothing to do with their marketing. As long as you have the reserves and the exploration, it takes some major mistakes not to make money or to be subjected to shareholder pressures. But the quality of marketing can indeed be seen in the down cycles.

What has been the problem with US automobile companies?

It's criminal because again, for the last 30 years, we have known all the issues. It's all about the size of the cars in the USA, oil consumption, reliability, manufacturing efficiency, services. These companies have shown a total inability to adapt and sustain change. In Europe, if you wanted to close down a plant of 10,000 workers, it would be impossible. By comparison, the USA doesn't have the excuse of rigid regulations and labour problems.

Yet, despite such flexibility in the system, General Motors and Ford have become fossilized because of their size, their culture, and – although they spend a fortune in advertising – have got it wrong. If you want to see an illustration of expensive and ineffective marketing, take a look at both of them.

So which companies would you consider to be good marketing performers?

There are three categories. The first is modern technology, fantastic companies with real marketing expertise, like Google, Skype, etc. These represent modern marketing at its best as they went directly from no marketing to good marketing in a competitive environment. They haven't been infested by the virus of bad marketing.

Once a company is infested by this virus, with marketers focusing on what's new and how to get more resources, it's very hard to get rid of it because internal politics within marketing departments means that people make alliances. You have to wait for a big crisis for change to occur.

Then you've got the big, bold marketers who still manage to be fantastic at marketing. Like L'Oréal, which to my mind hasn't suffered much in the last 20 years, and the new P&G, which suffered in the late 1990s but has made a fantastic comeback. It's also worth looking at what Beiersdorf has done with Nivea. I'm talking about big companies that are marketing professionals. There aren't that many at that level.

What is the last category?

This covers people who have invented new business models, and here I'd like to propose two examples. They are both fantastic. The first is Virgin and Richard Branson, but it is not only Branson as an individual, but the fact that he has been able to clone himself.

He has gone beyond making money – he has changed the world. His empire would still survive if he fell under a bus because he has created business models that are different. Virgin is not just an airline that is doing the same thing as other airlines, only better. It's doing it in a totally different way.

My other example is Commerce Bank, an American bank based in New Jersey. It's a totally new concept – it doesn't have branches but stores. It's not based on a banking model, but on McDonald's. It's only small, not a P&G, but it's fantastic and runs to something like 400 stores.

Getting more personal

What do you think it was about you that actually made you decide to travel the road you have?

I think, at the start, I was doing things for my own egotistical pleasure – the opposite of what I teach today, which is to be customer-oriented. I really enjoyed doing things I was passionate about. That was the first phase.

The next one – and I think this would be true for many people, entrepreneurs and the like – is that my career came about as a series of happy accidents. It happens. You do something for passion, yet often if you want to do it for money, arming yourself with a plan and a strategy, the whole thing doesn't work.

Many entrepreneurs are driven by passion. Some fail and some meet a happy accident. Mine was not my mainstream research, but Markstrat. It led me to Nestlé, General Electric, L'Oréal, and Reckitt & Colman, which was a fantastic time for me.

Then, third, it's a matter of why companies liked me. If I had to put this into words, I'd say this was my mix of vision and pragmatism. Very often I'm more pragmatic than the business people I meet. Maybe it's because I come from a modest family, from the Pyrenean mountains, where people have to struggle to survive.

It could be that the combination of coming from a modest family, life in the Pyrenees, my initial training as an engineer coupled with having to do loads of jobs to pay for my studies had an impact. I worked in hotels, restaurants, in South Wales, in London and other places around the world – all this is what has made me as I am.

And what are the qualities which you bring to what you do?

People see that I'm quite coherent and that I practise what I teach and preach. If they see me for a day, a week, six months or three years later, I'll still have the same principles. I may have evolved in terms of the knowledge and what I've tested and so on, but I'll still have the same principles.

There are a lot of smoke and mirrors in this industry. Frankly, I've never had time for that. Of course, I'll try to put on a nice suit and tie, to be pleasant and polite, and I don't always say what I think because sometimes it will upset people. But I can be careful, yet still honest. And I think people like that in the long term. That's why I've kept some clients for more than 20 years.

> *There are a lot of smoke and mirrors in this industry. Frankly, I've never had time for that. Of course, I'll try to put on a nice suit and tie, to be pleasant and polite, and I don't always say what I think because sometimes it will upset people. But I can be careful, yet still honest. And I think people like that in the long term.*

What are you proudest of in terms of your work?

I'm most proud of the help and influence I've had on people, companies and the world in which we live in a very modest way. When I meet people I haven't seen for 20 years, and they still have great memories of what I did with them, there's no bigger joy. So many people have said that their career has changed because of me. I'm not saying that happens for everybody I meet or teach, but the fact that it happens for a certain percentage of people with whom I've interacted is a fantastic source of energy.

Selected publications

Marketing Strategy: A Decision-Focused Approach, McGraw-Hill/Irwin, 5th edn 2006. Co-authors: John Mullins, Orville Walker and Boyd Harper.

Marketing Management: A Strategic Decision-Making Approach, McGraw-Hill/Irwin, 5th edn 2005. Co-authors: John Mullins, Orville Walker and Boyd Harper.

Markstrat On-Line: The Strategic Marketing Simulation, StratX. 2005. Co-author: Hubert Gatignon.

'Beyond Strategy: Market-based Capabilities', *Business: The Ultimate Resource*, Perseus Publishing, Cambridge USA and Bloomsbury Publishing, UK, 2002.

'Corporate Leadership in the New Economy', *The Salamander Link, INSEAD Alumni Association Magazine*, France, January, 2000.

The Report on the Competitive Fitness of Global Firms, Financial Times Prentice Hall, London, 1998, 1999, 2000, 2001, 2002.

Markstrat 3, The Strategic Marketing Simulation, Southwestern, 1997. Co-author: Hubert Gatignon.

Industrat™*: The Strategic Industrial Marketing Simulation*, Prentice-Hall College Division, 1988. Co-author: David Weinstein.

4

....

Regis McKenna

The technology visionary

Regis McKenna founded his own high tech marketing firm, Regis McKenna, Inc., in Silicon Valley in 1970 after working in the marketing departments of two early semiconductor pioneering companies. Over the past 30 years, his firm evolved from one focused on high tech start-ups to a broad-based marketing strategy firm servicing international clients in many different industries and countries. He retired from consulting in 2000 and is concentrating his efforts on high tech entrepreneurial seed-ventures (www.mckennas.com).

He is responsible for helping to launch some of the most important technological innovations of the last 26 years including the first microprocessor (Intel Corporation), the first personal computer (Apple Computer), the first recombinant DNA genetically engineered product (Genentech, Inc.), and the first retail computer store (The Byte Shop). Other first-time technology marketing efforts he participated in include the first commercial laser for retail systems, the first computer local area network, the first electronic spreadsheet, the first operating system for personal computers, the first mini supercomputer and the first desktop publishing system.

He has worked with a number of entrepreneurial start-ups during their early formative years including: America Online, Apple, Businessland, Electronic Arts, Genentech, Intel, Linear Technology, Microchip, Microsoft, 3COM, Tandem and many others. He has consulted on strategic marketing and business issues to many of the largest technology-based firms in the USA, Japan and Europe. And he continues to be involved in high tech start-up companies through his venture activities.

McKenna is included in the San Jose Mercury News' Millennium 100 *as one of the 100 people who made Silicon Valley what it is today. He has written and lectured extensively on the social and market effects of technological change, advancing innovations in marketing theories and practices. He has authored numerous books, including* The Regis Touch, Who's Afraid of Big Blue?, Relationship Marketing, Real Time: Preparing for the Age of the Never Satisfied Customer *and* Total Access: Giving Customers What They Want in an Anytime, Anywhere World. *He also sits on a number of boards in both the private and nonprofit sectors.*

The professional journey

You are known for so many things. Is there any area in particular you feel is associated with your name?

I suspect it is associated with helping a number of entrepreneurial companies create new product categories and, as a result, achieve rapid growth. My firm provided 'outsource marketing' strategy and services to a number of entrepreneurial start-ups in their earliest stages. Companies that – to use Steve Jobs' prescient comment made some 25 years ago – 'changed the world'. These include Apple, 3COM, Electronic Arts, Intel – perhaps the most recognized, but there were many others which have subsequently become globally recognized brands.

However, 'right time' and 'right place' had a great deal to do with whatever success I have had over the years. I was fortunate to have started my marketing career here in the Valley some 40 years ago. During those four decades, I was in the right place to participate in the introduction of several revolutionary technologies and observe them move from research and development (R&D) to market.

This included the microprocessor, personal computer, packaged software applications, biotech products and many others that have had a dramatic impact not only on business processes but also on consumer behaviour. Certainly not all new technologies came from Silicon Valley, but the Valley created a unique cultural environment that offered entrepreneurs a living laboratory for their ideas. My career spanned a lot of different technologies and industries as well as different economic and social environments.

The entrepreneurial culture of Silicon Valley influenced my views of marketing as well. After all, in the 1960s and 1970s, the old industries were losing out to the new. Foreign competition was also hollowing our American industries with new lower cost production methods, and marketing methods had become stagnant. I had a brief experience working for the old-line company Philco-Ford in the 1960s when Philco acquired the start-up where I was employed. I soon found myself trapped in a bureaucratic maze. An 'initiative' or a new idea required a full page of signatures before proceeding!

Entrepreneurial companies were not seen as capable of contributing to the economy. I well recall a 1970s financial analyst's report stating that new technologies, new products and services were not going to come from small companies but rather from divisions of major corporations because they had the resources required to be successful. Major financial publications would not write about technology companies unless they were public and on the New York Stock Exchange. One company dominated the computer world and that was IBM.

Today, it is difficult to imagine that companies such as Intel, Apple, Adobe, Cisco, 3COM, Electronic Arts, Genentech, Intuit and Microsoft were once struggling young businesses trying to educate the world about an entirely new way to do things – improve productivity, solve problems, do work, educate or be entertained. And yet, not so very long ago, they were trying to convince the world that they were real – they were the future. Silicon Valley companies encouraged an egalitarian environment where tenure and title didn't count as much as your ideas and performance. That formula proved to be highly successful.

Today, from smart phones, laptops and real-time financial transactions, ATMs and digital cameras to electronic games, medical instrumentation and even the internet – they all have a common ground in silicon. That's the stuff chips are made of and from which the new digital world took flight. Over the past 40 years, I travelled along with the technology evolution from chips to personal computers, to personal software and electronic retailing, to networks, application services, VoIP (voice over internet protocol) and now nanotech. So to have been in at the beginning, when it was just emerging and the marketplace was unaware of what was possible, and to participate in its evolution was fun, fascinating and enlightening. It was my MBA and PhD in how you move innovation from idea to market. And it is still a work in progress.

What made you move to Silicon Valley from the east coast of the USA?

I went to work for a technology publisher out of college and worked in a variety of jobs including copy-editing, production and sales. I was then asked to open the company's west coast office. I was young, recently married and we had few possessions to tie us down. My wife and I thought we would give it a try. We made our decision while my boss was waiting for an answer on the phone and moved to the San Francisco Bay Area within a few weeks.

I was raised and attended school in Pittsburgh, Pennsylvania, in the late 1940s and 1950s. For most of the first half of the 20th century, Pittsburgh was known as the 'steel capital' of the world. By the late 1950s, however, the old industrial era began to fade, jobs were hard to come by and visions of the high tech future, at least for me, were not on the horizon. I did not realize until some years later that the move to California was, for me, a transition from the industrial age to the information age.

So the whole concept of Silicon Valley was just beginning?

Yes. In fact, the name 'Silicon Valley' was not used until some years later. The integrated circuit co-invented by Bob Noyce at Fairchild a few years before was just beginning to ship small volumes of devices. Companies such as Intel, Apple and Genentech were yet to open their doors and many of the established technology companies such as Hewlett-Packard (HP) were not in the computer or printer business as yet. Most were developing products for defence and aerospace markets. Only a few large companies one might call high tech were located here and most of those have vanished – replaced by 'faster, better, cheaper' models from high tech start-ups. In fact, the term 'high tech' only came into popular use in the 1970s and 1980s. The term characterized a generational change – not only in the technologies but also in the way entrepreneurs leveraged R&D to create new markets and rapid growth.

And you were helping these young companies with their marketing?

When you say marketing, you must first understand my view of marketing. I learned marketing from hands-on experience. As a result, I wasn't biased by a formula or any preconceived text. Marketing is closing the loop. It is a process, not an event. I see marketing as continuing dialogue between the producer and the consumer whereby both learn, change and adapt. Marketing follows advances in technology, as history shows us. Mass production, radio, TV, computers, software and now the internet – all have led to innovative new approaches to marketing.

My primary teachers were my clients and their customers. While only a few individuals may have the title, marketing is every one's job. The best way I found both to educate myself and associates was to develop a network of knowledgeable people including 10 or 15 of our client's customers, or potential customers, in order to assess the perceptions and, if the product was in a trial, to ask: 'Does it meet or exceed expectations?' Internal audits became tools for building consensus. We often found that many of the company's managers and key players were operating with different objective and goals in mind.

In my experience, marketing and innovation work hand-in-hand. Revolutionary ideas and products are not like anything customers have seen or used before. They are not explicit replacements for existing products or services but rather something entirely new – a new way of doing work. So they force one to think about new ways to educate the consumer or to create new ways to engage them.

One has to try things, take risks as well as be creative, because there are no models or case studies to fall back on to emulate. New technology, for example, creates new markets and it also establishes a new language of the marketplace. Depending on the nature of the product, adoption often requires a completely new generation of users. That was true of the first microprocessor as well as the first personal computer. We see the same phenomenon with the initial users of Google and the iPod.

Had your background prepared you in any way for this?

Well, actually my formal education wasn't in marketing or business or technology, it was philosophy. However, I explored a lot of different subjects in college including economics, science, history and psychology. I thought I was preparing for a career in law school or possibly teaching. However, I enjoyed my science courses and I read a great deal about science and technology as well as social, cultural and science history.

Silicon Valley is addictive in the sense that it drives one to keep looking for the next big thing. Once caught up in it, you want to find out where it's heading. If you have any amount of curiosity about yourself, technology, the world around you or the future, you find yourself drawn to it and immersed in it.

While my peers were in graduate school or studying marketing, I had a wonderful opportunity to get my PhD inside the Valley's 'living classroom'. I spent at least half of my time in the field with sales organizations calling on customers. I travelled to Europe, opened offices in a number of different countries and that gave me an opportunity to work on engagements in different markets around the world. So it was a totally hands-on learning experience. I had one foot in the market and the other in technology development.

Silicon Valley is addictive in the sense that it drives one to keep looking for the next big thing. Once you find yourself caught up in it, you want to find out where it's heading. If you have any amount of curiosity about yourself, technology, the world around you or the future, you find yourself drawn to it and immersed in it.

Before you set up your own company, you worked in what were then some of the very young companies?

Yes, I joined the marketing department of General Micro Electronics (GMe) in 1965. An interesting aspect to this company was that this was my first experience seeing the end-to-end design and development of silicon to calculators. Although it was quite a primitive operation by modern standards, I was afforded an opportunity to learn a great deal about technology as well as the business of high tech. The company was relatively small, but in those days even small companies were vertically integrated. GMe grew the silicon ingots from molten silicon, sliced them into wafers, and did the photolithography and chip processing, packaging and testing under one roof. They designed the chips and did the circuit layouts as well.

Needless to say, watching the process in action and asking a lot of questions was my basic course in solid state engineering. The company began working on a new type of chip process called MOS (metal oxide silicon) that allowed for more devices on a chip. It also had lower power consumption than existing devices. The goal was to build computers for the US space program that were smaller in size and demanded fewer batteries to keep running. Along the way, the company began making desktop calculators from only 39 MOS chips for a large calculator company. This was a huge reduction in the number of components inside calculators and promised additional benefits of drastically increased reliability and lower-cost production.

Understand that the average price of a full function electromechanical calculator at the time was about the same as for the average family car! The media gave the company a lot of attention, but the process was not reliable and would not be capable of mass production until some years later. Only a relatively few calculators were produced and at such low volume that the cost was prohibitive and the program died. The company was then sold to Philco-Ford.

The technology was too early. The company was unable to implement and deliver the product. One has to know not only what is possible with any given technology but also to anticipate how unforgiving the market is when a promise leaves the customer empty-handed. For me, this was a seminal experience. Great idea. Poor execution. Six years later, Intel refined and developed the MOS process and launched the first microprocessor for a Japanese calculator company. It would be another 12 years before the Apple II hit the market with similar technology inside. Intel's first logo was 'Intel delivers'.

Then, in 1967, I went to National Semiconductor as marketing services manager. The west coast National spun out of Fairchild, as did most of the other chip companies in Silicon Valley.

It's hard to think of National Semiconductor as a tiny start-up, isn't it?

National was an old-line east coast transistor company which had financial problems and all but closed its door. Charlie Sporck and a handful of his trusted associates at Fairchild Semiconductor made a deal with the majority stockholder, Peter Sprague, and reopened the company in Silicon Valley. Don Valentine, vice president of marketing and sales, hired me and I joined a marketing department of four people including Don. The average age of a National employee was 35 years. National was an aggressive, fast-paced, no-nonsense company. The management fostered an egalitarian environment and I again had the opportunity to be involved in many parts of the business.

Don Valentine gave his direct reports a lot of freedom to operate but with heavy responsibility for outcomes. I often quipped that Don's philosophy was 'Do a good job and you can keep it'. (Don later went on to form Sequoia Capital, a leading venture firm in Silicon Valley. It backed Apple, Yahoo!, Google and Electronic Arts among many others.)

Under Don, I was able to travel a great deal of the time, meeting with distributors, sales reps, regional managers, industry analysts and the media. Later, when I started my own marketing firm, this approach became a standard 'external audit' process we used for getting perspective and perceptions on our clients' new products. Personally, I found the technical people in labs and engineering departments much more straightforward about their experiences with the new product than getting that information any other way.

Remember, this was before the internet and email. One had to get the information directly by travel and phone. Don's approach was very straightforward: know the customer; understand the business, the competitors and your products; and close the order. His whole approach was highly disciplined and demanding. For example, we had regular training sessions for sales people, even held exams. One of the courses he taught was 'how to read an annual report'. Don wanted reassurance that our customers were financially stable and able to pay their bills.

Don and Charlie never tolerated anyone sitting in their cubicle pushing papers. You were expected to be productive. Many people didn't like the tough Spartan culture at National but marketing was expected to perform and show results just like any other business operation. Intel under Andy Grove was much the same type of environment. Intel, however, integrated engineering and marketing much more closely. Both companies are still successful, albeit Intel spearheaded the digital revolution and became the world leader in chips.

But, even in the early days, chips began being designed into everything – cars, machine tools, games, TVs, traffic lights, medical devices, broadcast equipment, lunar landing vehicles – you name it. For me, starting in high tech, in a business that touched so many different industries and applications, and to be able to visit the companies that were just beginning to apply these new technologies to their particular applications, gave me a perspective that was invaluable.

If I can jump ahead for a minute, contrast that with today's world. In many organizations, one finds the rank and file of marketing people sitting in cubicles, isolated from all the various functions of the business. That means a marketing person is not necessarily exposed to every aspect of the company. As a result, few marketing people see how the pieces add up to the whole product. I encourage young marketing people to join young companies for just that reason. They better appreciate that marketing is everyone's job. When management sees it that way, they can leverage energies and ideas from every employee and every stakeholder. Apple and now Google are perhaps two shining examples of this approach today.

When you arrived, was Silicon Valley a much smaller place than it is now?

Yes, it was actually physically much smaller. It has grown geographically as well as in concept. Everything one needed was pretty much was within 50 square miles of Palo Alto. Venture capital, law and accounting firms, consultants, marketing firms – the entire supporting infrastructure developed around it. Universities such as University of California at Berkeley, Stanford, San Jose State and Santa Clara provided a steady supply of highly educated people as well as a steady flow of new ideas. The idea of Silicon Valley spawned dozens of geographic clones around the world.

Silicon Valley today has a highly diverse business base. As many as 50 different categories of business activity are located here, including biotech, medical instrumentation, software, communications, aerospace and a host of service industries. Venture capital has become a major business segment as well. The Bay Area gets the largest share of venture capital investment of any geographic area in the world.

You then started your own consultancy in 1970. When did you start to firm up the ideas for which you are now so well known, such as building customer relationships?

From my previous comments, you can see that ideas derive from past experiences that developed over time. I was in an environment where one is constantly challenged by new opportunities. Silicon Valley was a network of relationships long before the internet became a means of connecting. The concepts of my book *Relationship Marketing* came from looking closely at the way successful new companies leveraged their market infrastructure – beta customers, alliances, channel partners, research organizations, suppliers, media, venture and finance stakeholders and so forth – to build support for new technologies and products.

As the industry began to move more aggressively into computers and software, many hardware executives found they had to work well in advance and more closely with software developers because the software adds so much value to the final solution. Every layer or new platform of technology adds another layer of relationships that are necessary for a high tech business to leverage other developers' assets and get to market acceptance fast.

Customers, particularly at the enterprise level, use many different types of computers and software programs and they want all this stuff to work in harmony. As a result, businesses form many cross-relationships in order to provide a complete and compatible solution.

Harvard's Michel Porter said that every industry has an infrastructure that makes it unique. The management that wants to be successful has to learn what makes its particular infrastructure tick. In other words, every industry is a Rubik's cube of interdependent layers of relationships. Innovative companies often build entirely new infrastructures with new combinations of players. Essentially, that has been my driver: to figure out what it takes to build new infrastructures for innovative technology products and services.

Weren't you writing about the role of networks well before the internet? Did you see it coming?

I was very much into the idea of networking, but the internet had its own path of development and only went commercial in about 1994. I was an early user of online technology connecting my office and my home via modems, but that was about it. The development of various enabling software components such HTML and TCP/IP and the browser interface to interpret it all was an offshoot of US government defence spending.

In the early 1960s the US Department of Defense Advanced Research Projects Agency initiated the idea of developing a communication network – somewhat like a spider web – that could be operable even if partially destroyed by a nuclear attack. Remember, this was the Cold War era. The Agency's funding stimulated research in a number of government contractors, including several leading technical universities. The internet was on its own path of revolution.

On another path, plain old telephones lines and modems were used to connect the first hobby or personal computers. In the late 1970s Hayes Microcomputer of Atlanta, Georgia, developed the first low-cost modem that could be controlled by the personal computer to access the phone line and send data streams back and forth between computers. Hayes was an early client of ours. A few years later another client, America Online, began building an infrastructure based on a network of modems and providing users access to their various services such as chat rooms and interactive games. Chat rooms were somewhat like group therapy sessions!

Meanwhile, Bob Metcalfe left Xerox Parc, where he developed Ethernet, a technology for sending data at high speed over coaxial cable, and formed 3COM – yet another start-up client. By the time the internet went commercial in around 1994, the idea of communicating via one's personal computer was fairly well established. There is more to Silicon Valley's participation in the commercialization of the internet but that story has been told. Suffice to say that the idea of networking was ingrained in the Silicon Valley culture. The Apple II and the PC, together with low-cost modems, empowered people to talk to one another, moving beyond the machine-to-machine mainframe communications. Little wonder the internet was adopted and grew so rapidly.

One of your seminal articles was 'Marketing is Everything' in the _Harvard Business Review_ in 1991. Is it just as relevant today?

More so. All business activity today has become increasingly complex and at the same time is faced with the need for real-time information. The business environment is also more competitive and, of course, global. The American auto industry never quite caught on to this idea. Toyota and Honda found that, by focusing on building quality into their cars and having everyone in the business be responsible for every step of the process, from sourcing components to service, they could capture Ford and GM's home market. That is effective marketing. One can double the amount of advertising spent and provide interest-free loans but those types of marketing activity will not deliver a reliable, dependable driver experience.

Marketing is not only about advertising. My experience tells me that marketing is best accomplished when it is approached as a multidisciplinary business activity. Quality was once thought of as a specific corporate function. That all changed in the 1980s, when total quality management programs in Japan taught American companies the benefits of having all employees engaged in the process of product quality, feedback from customers and continued incremental improvement. Marketing is rapidly becoming a technology and many marketing people still see it as an art. Customer relationship management (CRM) was designed and developed by software engineers, not marketing consultants or ad agencies.

Distribution, once a department of most marketing organizations, is now logistics. Logistics is a network of services coordinated by software programs with the idea of efficient delivery of goods and services to the customer's doorstep. Most businesses could not efficiently run any part of their business today without computers, software and high speed networks. Coordinating resources, inventories and moving products from the click of a mouse to production and doorstep delivery, when done efficiently with all the proper notifications to the customer, is also good marketing.

I think marketing, as a function, has lost much of its position and power because the responsibility for many of the marketing functions is already dispersed throughout the enterprise. The chief information officer (CIO) and information professionals keep the communications networks and customer access channels up and running 24/7/365. In many organizations, the vice president of business development reports directly to the chief executive officer (CEO), as does the vice president of logistics.

While doing research on my book, *Total Access*, I spoke with quite a few executives running operations, logistics, IT and business development. None claimed a marketing title but all used terms such as 'customer care', 'brand building', 'customer life cycle' and 'service'. I like this trend! It makes businesses more customer-friendly and more successful. And in the last analysis, the CEO is the chief marketing officer because he or she is the only one with the power and responsibility to coordinate all the resources within an enterprise to make big changes happen.

You've also written that the CIO is taking over more of marketing as technology becomes so central to a company's performance.

I think the CIO is doing much of the marketing already. The CIO is the one who has to manage the nerve centre of the marketing enterprise. More than half of all marketing today in industries such as retail, financial services, travel and on-demand entertainment is done by software and network systems. Think about it. Research, datamining, customer life-cycle management, segmentation, self-service, market simulation, sales lead management, key word and embedded ads and CRM are all new high tech tools for better marketing effectiveness. The CIO and information professionals are the people who make sure that all those information resources are current and available on demand.

And with increasing identity thefts, illegal computer access and fraud, the CIO's responsibility for assuring customer privacy is yet another way of providing customer care satisfaction.

When you started writing about these ideas in your books and articles, did you get the reaction you hoped to?

Well, yes and no. People interpreted the word 'marketing' in many different ways. Some associate the function of marketing with sales, some with various forms of promotion. The word 'brand' is used so casually today that I think it has lost its meaning. My views are that good marketing is not the result of any of the cosmetic factors of 'image' and 'brand', but rather the net result of many different and diverse talents within a business. Further, that the discipline of marketing – if one can call it a discipline – changes with new generations and eras of technology.

With the internet, marketing with the old model of broadcast has been replaced by access. Pushing messages out to an impassive audience is not the way the internet is being used. The internet is interactive and engaging. I don't propose a lot of answers or 'how to' approaches. The technology and consumer adaptation to it is happening so fast that I feel it is important to develop new paradigms of marketing – marketing that is real-time, constantly in touch, responding and adapting dynamically.

It may be a few years off before we see this as a common marketing phenomenon but, if one looks closely, we will see it gradually coming into practice. In my two recent books, *Total Access* and *Real Time*, I tried to show the subtle effects of technology on consumer and market behaviour. I also tried to give my readers a way to think about the rapidly changing and expanding digital marketplace. Technology isn't slowing down to wait for those who don't get it. Marketing has some catching up to do.

And even though you formally retired from consultancy in 2000, you are still involved in helping companies?

I'm still very much connected to a number of venture capital firms. And I am a partner in a small, high tech, seed investment firm. We invest in a few emerging technology businesses and try to help them in the early stages.

Sometimes we help them write their business plans, do competitive analysis, assist in developing venture capital, give a bit of business advice – whatever the particular start-up needs in order to be successful.

So in a way you have come full circle?

In a way. It's a cumulative history and I am always referring to past experiences as lessons for going forward. When I'm in meetings with some of the companies whose boards I sit on, I almost feel apologetic when I start telling stories from 10 or 20 years ago that they can learn from. But I have to be careful, because I don't want the entrepreneurs to copy what others have done, but rather take the idea to a new level by adding their own creative touches. Copying other companies' approaches doesn't lead to a distinctive market position.

Current views of marketing

What's your overall view of the marketing profession at the moment?

Marketing is doing very well. My own view is it's just not being done well by the marketing people. Marketers spend too much time on advertising and promotion. And while they are doing that, as I said before, the CIO is automating their core functions. As they obsess over brand, the chief strategy officer is dispersing their responsibilities throughout the organization. And as they squabble over whether marketing is an art or a science, they're completely overlooking the fact that marketing has become a technology.

Marketing is doing very well. My own view is it's just not being done well by the marketing people. Marketers spend too much time on advertising and promotion. And while they are doing that . . . the CIO is automating their core functions. And as they squabble over whether marketing is an art or a science, they're completely overlooking the fact that marketing has become a technology.

Could you elaborate on that a bit?

For example, I think Google probably has more software PhDs in the company than marketing people. It changed the paradigm of how much of marketing is going to be done in the future.

Let me back up a bit. When radio was first introduced, it reached into the living space of consumers and it was free. But the content had to be paid for if radio was to become a viable medium. Broadcasters, on the other hand, had to find a way to finance the operation if their new venture was to be sustained. The internet faced the same question in its first few years of commercial operation: 'Who is going to pay for content?'

Initially, like radio, content on the internet was free. It's hard to sustain a business on 'free'. In the early 1930s, Procter & Gamble (P&G), maker of Ivory soap, began sponsoring a serial program for housewives called *Ma Perkins*. Such programs are referred to as the 'the soaps'. Advertising sponsorship became a practice that has since turned into a multibillion-dollar business. Broadcast technology made it possible and P&G, a great marketing company, was smart enough to adopt the new medium quickly. That changed the nature of advertising and made radio, and TV for that matter, a viable marketing medium.

Google is doing the same thing only in a different era and with a new medium, the internet. It is using its technology to connect consumers and producers. Ad messages are embedded within the text or interactive page so that the consumer can respond within the context of the article or ad with a click of the mouse. The consumer can search for whatever product or service they want and click to link to an online store, make a purchase or just get more information. The logistics within the network take it from there and manage the entire process from click to delivery and warrant registration.

On the other hand, the internet also links the consumer to the whole competitive framework of choices for any one product or service. Robert Putnam, author of *Bowling Alone*, sees the online consumer's relationships as transient – too easy to enter and too easy to exit. He refers to the experience as a 'drive-by relationship'. Using the internet to build consumer loyalty is a new phenomenon and I suspect the communication tools will evolve and change as businesses gain more experience with the medium. I don't think the marketing world has quite grasped the whole phenomenon of real-time consumer choice and on-demand service.

Consumers are coming into the marketplace via the internet and changing their buying habits. One billion people have access to the Internet. It's a global phenomenon. But the noise level is high. And even though there's a high rate of junk mail, spam, pop-ups, phishing, and the like, consumer traffic on the internet is expanding. What marketers haven't quite figured out yet is how to build a lasting, loyal relationship with consumers with this new medium.

Are companies like Google rewriting the rules?

Yes, I think they are in many different ways. Advertising agencies, for example, are trying to figure out their role in this new medium. At present, online advertising is a small percentage of overall expenditures. However, online advertising is growing more rapidly than broadcast and print. Google goes direct to the sponsors and the sponsors to Google. As this medium becomes more popular, the value of the advertising agency decreases. Online advertising is directly measurable.

Traditional forms of advertising have long searched for accurate measurement tools. The role of creative people is still important, very important, but an ad agency often stifles creativity and one finds that when large agencies become part of conglomerates they don't seem to use their combined resources to explore emerging technology tools. Print and broadcast advertising and its role in brand building hit a peak in the heydays of television. The computer and your smart phone will soon be your TV screen as well.

We see more diverse ways to reach the consumer, but the messages are lost in the noise and chaos. And I suspect that we will see more creative resources with a wider range of skills and talents offering creative software campaigns. Creative people are going to have to learn how to use this new medium. We will also see more advertising agencies becoming 'software companies'. Several years ago, I gave a talk to the executive management team at P&G. In the Q&A session, I was asked by one of the executives, 'Will our future ad agency be a software company?'

What other companies do you rate?

There are quite a few: Apple, Intel, IBM, Starbucks, FedEx, Intuit and Toyota. I've read quite a bit about the UK-based retailer Tesco whose management understands how to use the technology to service its customers where other grocery retailers have failed. I also think Starbucks is a phenomenal concept and company. It invests a great deal in information technology but what makes it successful is location, location, location. It has become a cultural phenomenon.

What companies do you feel have stood the test of time?

Obviously, there are any number of companies that have been around for 50, even 100 years – P&G, Coca-Cola, Pepsi, Ford and General Motors. Here in Silicon Valley, the biggest company is still HP and it was founded in 1940. HP seems to have had its share of problems over the past decade but, like most large companies, it needed to rethink who it was after the founders passed on.

Intel has certainly passed the test of time. It was founded a year after National in 1968. It has had its difficult periods in the past but has always succeeded by investing heavily in R&D. Oracle, AMD, Cisco, Electronic Arts, Genentech, Yahoo!, Applied Materials, 3COM and others have sustained difficult periods, rebounded and continue to perform well.

A Silicon Valley company which is not as visible but has done extremely well for its investors and customers is Linear Technology. It has sustained profitability quarter after quarter for the past 20 years. IBM has a large presence here in the Valley, as does Microsoft and other non-California-based companies. Quite a few have been around for 20 years or more. But no one feels content because everyone knows how fragile the leadership in any technology is and how fickle consumers can be when a new idea hits the market.

I wrote *Who's Afraid of Big Blue?* in 1988 and looked at what was going wrong at IBM. Many people thought Digital Equipment would displace IBM as the leader in enterprise computing. In my book, I said then that small companies such as Microsoft, Apple, Compaq and others were nibbling them to death. Lou Gerstner arrived and brought the company back to life. He set about regaining the company's leadership and transformed it into a services company with a strong research base.

Recently, IBM Research began exploring the science of services. Consider that the service economies have become the dominant economic contributor to GDP and the growth of GDP, not only in the US economy but for most of the modern industrial nations as well. And now over half of IBM's business is based on software and services. That transition from primarily a mainframe company to a software and services company has been dramatic. It's now the world's largest business and technology services company.

Apple – well, what can one say that hasn't been said about Steve Jobs and Apple? The company had a glorious birth and childhood; fell into the dark ages only to emerge after 10 years as a born-again innovative company. Apple is 30 years young.

Do you feel optimistic about marketing as opposed, perhaps, to marketers?

Marketing is in the midst of tremendous change – perhaps more significant change than we have seen since the advent of radio and television broadcasting. Consider digital technology, the internet, search engines, software tools and applications, blogs, social networks, broadband, WiFi, Bluetooth, VoIP, on-demand services, MP3 players and smart phones. Consumers are connected 24/7.

IT costs are rising and the demand for real-time information by management, suppliers and customers is increasing. Competitive pressure and the need to be ever more productive is driving companies to keep existing customers and develop new growth markets. China, India and Brazil are looked to for the next three billion consumers. Suddenly the world of communications got bigger and more complex.

I'm optimistic because there's a tremendous amount of interest in marketing. Sometimes when we speak with companies their first notion is to think of marketing in terms of branding or getting attention in the media. But instant success takes time. Infrastructures are not built overnight and management has to learn by adapting. One has to build an efficient, customer-friendly infrastructure to make it happen.

As I said before, marketing is being integrated into many corporate responsibilities. However, one might not call what they are doing marketing. None the less, they are serving the customer.

Are there any tips that you can offer to help people struggling to become excellent at marketing?

I visited a new company recently and was asked by the management to help develop 'a message' for its new product and service. I tend to cringe when I am asked that question. I like to see management focus first on customer needs and the competitive obstacles. I like to see the product evaluated by knowledgeable beta users and get feedback. I asked, what's missing that decreases value in the customer's experience? I like to see a product that is complete enough so that management has confidence in its ability to deliver on customer expectations.

By asking a lot of questions and mapping out the issues and missing pieces, we ended up not creating a message but rather going back to do more work on the whole product: one that they can be assured will get high marks from the first customers. Positioning comes from the marketplace and the customers, not a consultant's conference room.

The answer to your question is – keep asking questions. Never stop looking for better, more creative and productive ways to help your company or develop customer relationships. Learn about the new tools for dialogue with the marketplace and the customer. There are no 10 steps to marketing greatness. Greatness comes from forging your own path and that takes learning from your experiences.

Getting more personal

Is there a moment in your life you consider a defining time, something that set you on the path that you're now on?

That's an easy one. The move to California. Even though I wasn't of the technology world, when I began to visit the companies and develop relationships here in the Valley and extend those to many parts of the high tech marketplace, I found a willingness of people to exchange ideas openly and a willingness to educate me about the technology they were developing. Over time, my own ideas emerged and, because I had developed many relationships in the technology community, I was able to exchange ideas and views. I continue to do that today.

Sounds like fun.

It was. It has been an absolute joy. I always liked to hang around labs in universities and companies because the lab is where you see all the new stuff emerging.

What do you think it is about you that got you so involved in all this?

Curiosity. I think that it's been an important factor driving me. I mentioned before that the technology is addictive. If you visit Silicon Valley you'll find many people who keep pursuing the future even though they have the means to spend the rest of their lives on a beach. You work even though you're successful enough not to work simply because the technology keeps saying: 'Here's another way to move into the future.'

What do you reckon you are proudest of in terms of what you've done?

What do I look back upon with the most pride? From a business and marketing perspective, I was fortunate to be located here in Silicon Valley at a time when hundreds of entrepreneurial companies were being formed each year. I have much pride in being part of the early marketing efforts for many of those pioneering companies whose founders and technologies launched the digital information age. Many of the companies and their products have subsequently become established global brands.

I have much pride in being part of the early marketing efforts for many of those pioneering companies whose founders and technologies launched the digital information age. Many of the companies and their products have subsequently become established global brands.

Few marketing people have had the privilege to know and work with entrepreneurs such as Bob Noyce (founder of Intel and inventor of the microchip), Gordon Moore and Andy Grove (Intel), Steve Jobs (Apple),

Bob Metcalfe (3COM), Bob Swanson and Herb Boyer (Genentech) and many, many others who are perhaps not as well known but nonetheless key individuals responsible for fundamental innovations essential for building the information age infrastructure.

I had the best teachers. Entrepreneurs such as those I mention above viewed my marketing resources as integral to the success of their companies. I have a lot of pride in having developed lasting relationships with so many interesting people from all parts of the world and being actively engaged in the flowering of the information age.

Selected publications

Total Access: Giving Customers What They Want in an Anytime, Anywhere World, Harvard Business School Press, 2002.

Real Time: Preparing for the Age of the Never Satisfied Customer, Harvard Business School Press, 1997.

Relationship Marketing: Successful Strategies for the Age of the Customer, Addison-Wesley, 1992.

Who's Afraid of Big Blue? How Companies are Challenging IBM – and Winning, Addison-Wesley, 1988.

The Regis Touch: New Marketing Strategies for Uncertain Times, Addison-Wesley, 1985.

Over the years McKenna has also published countless articles challenging accepted wisdom in journals and magazines around the world.

5

....

Don Peppers and Martha Rogers

The one-to-one gurus

The names Don Peppers and Martha Rogers PhD are synonymous with the idea of dealing with customers one-to-one. They kicked off what became the customer relationship management (CRM) revolution and changed the landscape of business competition with their classic bestseller, The One to One Future, *in 1993. They are now considered leading authorities on customer-focused strategies for business.*

Both of them consistently appear on lists of influential business thinkers and intellectuals, while they are in great demand around the world as speakers. Together they have co-authored a series of international best sellers which have collectively sold well over a million copies in 17 languages.

Other books include: Enterprise One to One *(1997), which shows how CRM strategies and interactive marketing should be applied differently in different business situations;* The One to One Fieldbook *(1999), co-authored with their business partner Bob Dorf, a step-by-step guide to the mechanics of Peppers & Rogers Group's methodology for building customer relationships and* The One to One Manager *(1999), which highlights the pioneers who dared to implement one-to-one strategies.* One to One B2B: Customer Development Strategies for the Business-to-Business World *(2001) provides detailed case studies on five major corporations that embraced a vision for the B2B customer relationship.*

The authors have also published the first-ever CRM textbook for university use in graduate level courses, Managing Customer Relationships *(2004). Their most innovative strategic thinking is embodied in their newest book,* Return on Customer, *released in 2005. This book bridges the gap between marketing and finance, proposing a new metric (ROC^{sm}) for tracking the efficiency with which customers create economic value for a business and tying it directly to total shareholder return.*

In addition, Peppers is the author of Life's a Pitch – Then You Buy, *based on his career as a new business rainmaker for world-class advertising agencies, including Chiat/Day and Lintas:USA. He capped his advertising career as the chief executive officer (CEO) of Perkins/Butler Direct Marketing, a top-20 US direct marketing agency.*

Prior to marketing and advertising, he worked as an economist in the oil business and as the director of accounting for a regional airline. He holds a BSc in astronautical engineering from the US Air Force Academy, and a master's degree in public affairs from Princeton University's Woodrow Wilson School.

Rogers started writing advertising copy in her senior year at university, which she continued to do while pursuing an MA in English. Advertising interested her to such an extent that she decided to study for another MA. The university was so impressed by her experience that she ended up teaching a course instead, while being fast-tracked onto the doctorate program as a Bickel Fellow. She then spent 15 years teaching marketing at Bowling Green State University in Ohio, departing in 1995 as a full professor.

She is now, among other posts, an adjunct professor at the Fuqua School of Business at Duke University, as well as the co-director of the Customer Relationship Management Center at Duke. She is widely published in academic and trade journals, including the Journal of Advertising Research, *the* Journal of Public Policy and Marketing, Harvard Business Review *and the* Journal of Applied Psychology.

Together they are founding partners of Peppers & Rogers Group, a leading customer-focused management consulting firm, with clients in a variety of industries and offices on five continents. In August 2003, Peppers & Rogers Group joined Carlson Marketing Worldwide to provide clients with world-class customer strategy.

The professional journey

What, in your view, are you best known for?

Martha: I think that it's probably true that we're best known for one-to-one, for building customer relationships and growing customer value.

Don: I agree: one-to-one marketing – which became CRM, really.

When did you write your first book?

Don: 1993. It was *The One to One Future*, which was about building relationships one customer at a time. Which is what customer relationship management is all about, of course. And what's interesting about our first book was that it was not at all an instant hit. It was a very, very slow build. We sold more books in 1995 than we did in 1993 or 1994.

Why do you think that was?

Don: The reason was the internet arrived. Once people started building websites, they realized they could have direct, very inexpensive, interactive relationships – real connections with their customers. And what should they do with this? The answer was: build relationships the way we had suggested, which was now possible with these new technologies.

Martha: I think that's right. I will tell you something else interesting that happened in 1995. It was some time during that summer. Don was off travelling somewhere and I was off travelling somewhere else. And we each got phone calls from several journalists who said to us: 'Well, did you hear that today IBM announced that it is starting a consulting practice in customer relationship management? Doesn't that just make you mad because that's sort of invading your turf?'

And even though we hadn't spoken with each other, we said the same thing, which was: 'No, we think it's cool, it's great, because two years ago people thought that we were nuts to suggest that you could have individual relationships with your customers. And now only two years later here's IBM, Big Blue, mainstreaming the idea.'

Don: When we started out, you couldn't get arrested talking about relationships.

Martha: Yeah, people thought we were crazy.

Did you actually use the phrase 'customer relationship management' in your first book?

Don: We didn't use the term.

Martha: Not that phrase, no.

Don: What we did use was the term 'relationship management'. We might have actually used the words 'customer relationship management' at some point or customer relationship marketing or managing customer relationships, but we called it 'one-to-one' marketing for a purpose. And that was because there was already a fairly well-developed repertoire of marketing wisdom around the whole idea of relationship marketing.

In fact, Regis McKenna had published his book *Relationship Marketing* in 1991 and we wanted to differentiate ourselves from that because what we were talking about was somewhat different. We were not talking about building a relationship with a population of customers through a general increase in the level of service, but about literally treating different customers differently. So we used the term 'one-to-one marketing' to capture that concept.

> *We called it 'one-to-one' marketing for a purpose . . . We were not talking about building a relationship with a population of customers through a general increase in the level of service, but about literally treating different customers differently. So we used the term 'one-to-one marketing' to capture that concept.*

Martha: At first, we did talk about the ability to think about customers and portfolios and about the idea of managing customers, not products. And so, in that sense, we talked about customer management, calling it 'customer portfolio management'. Even now, we don't like to use the term CRM very much, so it's OK with us that other people have used that term.

Don: And keep in mind that the people who did introduce the term CRM were doing it primarily in order to take a creative shortcut for talking about a whole range of software applications.

Which of you came up with the phrase 'one-to-one', or was that a sort of mutual 'light bulb'?

Don: Everything we do is mutual.

You both came up with it?

Don: Simultaneously in our sleep on the same day.

Martha: At the same moment.

But actually?

Don: Seriously, we never talk about who comes up with what. That would be the end of our friendship. Right, Martha?

Martha: Well, there's that, but there's also, as in any brainstorming, how do you really separate it out?

What impact did your respective backgrounds in advertising have on the development of your thinking?

Martha: I think that's an excellent question and I'm going to tell you something. Don, by training, is an astronautical engineer, which means he really *is* a rocket scientist. This is true. And then he studied public policy and all of that sort of points naturally to a career in brand advertising. I'm being facetious of course.

Don: We used to sit around our college astronautics class trying to figure out a problem of orbital mechanics and, finally, somebody would scratch their head, stand up and say, 'Come on guys, this isn't advertising.'

Martha: Neither of us really trained for what we do. But the pair of us actually bring a lot of different stuff to the table. I have a liberal arts background and was an advertising copywriter whereas Don was more into the marketing management side. In addition to that, when I met Don he was living in New York City, so he brought the big city perspective. I lived not only in a small, rural university town, Bowling Green Ohio, but actually outside the town. So that gives me a completely different, small town perspective. And one of us is a woman, the other a man, which also makes a huge difference, and one of us is an academic and the other isn't. So I think that those multiple perspectives have been very helpful to us in our work and in our business.

Interesting. What was the wider context at the time when you came up with this concept?

Don: I remember this time very vividly because I was working in the advertising agency business and everyone was worried about the fragmentation of media. Media vehicles were proliferating. There were more and more television channels available on cable TV and the advertising agency world was watching this trend with increasing trepidation because it used to be so easy to make money in advertising.

You'd create a really good television commercial and you'd slap a $20-million TV campaign behind it and you'd put $3-million worth of commission in the bank. That's a pretty easy business model. Now we were talking about so many different channels and other media. And the world was increasingly awash in advertising. When we began writing the book you could dig up statistics like the fact that the average consumer in America was coming face to face with some 3,000 different promotional messages per day.

So, basically, it was like the advertising industry was in a state of suspense. It didn't really know what was going to happen and hoped that whatever technological innovation would bring, television interactivity into the home could be somehow harnessed to the benefit of advertising as an industry. But no one really knew how it would happen.

Did the recession of the early 1990s have any impact?

Don: There was indeed a recession in the early 1990s, but the truth is the recession had almost nothing to do with the way we wrote our book. We didn't write it based on the economic situation, but rather on the direction of technologies in data management, interactivity and mass customization.

Martha: It wasn't really about the economic reaction of companies at all. It was about what *would* have to happen, what *would* be forced on companies as a consideration of the technologies that were driving inexorably forward. Remember that, in 1984, just a few years before Don and I met in 1990, we saw the very first personal computer introduced by Apple.

And over the next few years we began to see these new computer brands that at the time could barely even run basic video games. This was very early on, when cell phones were still the size and weight of a brick and microwave ovens were new.

Don: And fax machines used thermal paper and cost $550 or more. Martha and I were both looking at this independently before we even met, but one of the things that particularly focused me on it occurred when I was still in the advertising business. I had the opportunity to do a speech that I couldn't get my media director to do, so I had to do it because I had booked the speech on behalf of the agency and it was on the impact of interactivity on marketing. And in those days, this is like mid-1989, interactivity was expected to arrive in about 20 years with fibre optic cable into the home, which would give homes 400 TV channels and a way, possibly, to interact with them.

So, in thinking through this and going through the literature I came up with a sort of thought experiment. I said: 'Let's suppose that a child could talk back to Tony the Tiger during a Kellogg's cornflakes commercial. What would Kellogg do with that child's input?' Well, if you think about it carefully, and look at the marketing model that drove the advertising and brand-building budgets at that time, the answer was they wouldn't do anything with that information because it wasn't representative; it was anecdotal. It would only be useful if it the child's feedback represented some kind of population or segment.

And yet my own job in the advertising world was winning new clients for my ad agency. So I spent a great deal of time trying to make contact with potential clients, have an interaction with them, take notes, remember what they said from last time, call them up again and ask how that product introduction had gone, or how the new campaign was working. The reason I wanted to talk to them was so that they would tell me things about their business and their problems so I could build a relationship. For me, this was the insight: that, when interactivity occurs, when it becomes possible to interact with customers, probably everyone is going to want to build relationships. I think Martha had more or less the same insight at about the same time, and it drove the writing of our book.

Martha: What happened was that I had been talking to my colleagues in the marketing department where I was a professor. All my students wanted the fictional job that Tom Hanks had in a film called *Nothing in Common*, where he played a successful ad guy. Of course, that job not only never really existed; it sure as heck doesn't exist now. But that's what they wanted to do. And I tried to explain to them that, sooner or later, TV advertising was going to be a lot less important than it was at the time. This was in 1990 and they didn't want to hear it. Finally, of course, even the packaged goods makers are transferring TV budgets into relationship building but, at the time, they all thought I was out of my mind.

So I was trying very hard to talk to people about this topic without much success. Then I went to this luncheon meeting and there was this guy from

New York with his little ponytail, because that was cool if you were on Madison Ave – I still rib Don about that – and here he was saying the stuff I was talking to these people about. And he was taking himself really seriously, too.

So I went up to him afterwards and said, 'There needs to be a book on this subject because nobody gets this.'

And he said, 'I'm sorry, I'm on Madison Ave, I don't have time to write a book.'

So I said, 'Well, I'm in the "publish or perish" business, so let's write this book together.'

After a five-minute conversation we shook hands and decided to write a book. That was seven books, countless articles, millions of miles, and a whole company ago.

Don: Next we began faxing each other.

Martha: We did. When we wrote this first book there was no email yet. We had email on the academic campus but there was no email for the real world and so each of us would work every day and then we would download everything on to a hard disk and then go over to the post office and mail it overnight.

Don: That, and we would fax pages and pages back and forth. It was fax torture.

What was it about that speech that led to the two of you joining forces?

Don: The reaction was quite interesting. Everybody thought it made logical sense, but they didn't really think that interactivity was just around the corner. And part of Martha's and my goal in *The One to One Future* was to portray an interactive future that really was right around the corner. If you look through our book now it reads like a book of business science fiction because all the examples are hypothetical. If I had a diaper company I would do this. If I had a car company, or an airline, or a bank . . . and so on.

Martha: What if . . . what if?

Don: What we tried to do is bring it home, with real world, interactive vehicles that were available to companies on a reasonably cost-efficient basis at that time, including something we called 'fax response' which never really took off because it was supplanted by the web so fast. But fax response is directly analogous to having a website. It's where you speed dial into a fax server and download whatever pages are stored there for you, almost exactly like downloading a web page. Of course when I gave that first speech, I didn't even know about fax response. But I remember one time I got a question – I can tell this story, right, Martha?

Martha: Sure.

Don: I got a question from the audience because I talked about how fax machines are interactive and what if you had a computer send those fax messages in different ways to different customers. Someone in the audience asked, 'Why, if only 5% of households have fax machines, would people do this?'

And I said, 'Well, what if an entrepreneur were to give people fax machines if they agreed to take some advertising and filled out a questionnaire?' and I thought, 'Hmm', and then I said, 'No, that will never happen.'

Then I went home and started writing the business plan for 'Home Fax' which also helped us, both Martha and me, develop our thinking on this because in wrestling through the mechanics of actually setting up an interactive service you have to deal with some of these issues.

Martha: What happens when the interactions with customers are so valuable it actually pays to *give* them the means to communicate?

Did you ever get annoyed that, when you were talking about these concepts, a lot of the software people were rushing around saying, 'Buy the software off the shelf and you'll be able to do CRM, this wonderful new thing'?

Martha: I'm laughing because that's why we're really hesitant to use the term 'customer relationship management' now, because the CRM term, we think, was really usurped by the people who were making that software and doing the technology. So what ended up happening was that those software salespeople were out in huge force, doing their job, saying, 'If you just buy the technology and put it in place then you're going to have a miraculous turnaround. You're going to have real relationships with your customers and it's going to be great.'

And so people did in fact spend $20m or $50m on the software. They installed it and, no matter how well that went, nothing happened. Because, for one-to-one to be successful, you had to make a lot of other fundamental changes in the company. Just having the technology in place wouldn't do it. It had to be linked to all the data about your customers, which was not always the case once it was all finished. And so, as a result, there was a backlash against CRM because that's the term that had been used by the software people and it became synonymous with software that's going to be a disappointment. But, happily, I think it's true that there was no backlash against the 'one-to-one' concept we were writing about.

The CRM term, we think, was really usurped by the people who were making that software and doing the technology . . . And so people did in fact spend $20m or $50m on the software. They installed it and, no matter how well that went, nothing happened. Because, for one-to-one to be successful, you had to make a lot of other fundamental changes in the company. Just having the technology in place wouldn't do it.

Don: That having been said, the software boom was very good for us. Many of those software companies, such as BroadVision, Epiphany, Teradata, SAP, SAS Institute and Oracle, wanted to make software sales, so they contracted a lot of speaking engagements with us to sort of prime the pump, to get people excited about what they could do if they just had the tools. For this reason we have mixed feelings, because I think we were partly responsible for the CRM hype.

Although we certainly were very careful to say in all our speeches that it takes a lot more than just the software, you've got to do this, this and this. But a lot of people just didn't hear that and, of course, the software people with the contracts in the back of the room didn't want them to hear it. Also, there was more money than God in those days. That was back in 1999, 2000.

And how long then before you set up the consultancy?

Don: Well, the truth is we only set up the consulting operation for real in the late 1990s, around 1998, 1999. In 1997 we had written *Enterprise One to One*. We had this vision of the interactive world and the more technology that came out, basically, the richer our vision became. By the late 1990s a lot of companies were beginning to talk about it. There were software firms that were launching products around building relationships. For example, there were companies that had named their software after us, like Broad-Vision's One-to-One application, for instance.

Didn't you copyright the term?

Don: We didn't copyright it. We wanted people to use it.

Martha: We ended up copyrighting a version of it after a long time. We were fine with other people using it, but we had been bitten a few times when some other phrases we had originated got picked up and service marked by others. So we wanted to make sure nobody else took ownership of the term.

Don: Yes, we got trademarks for 1TO1 and 1to1 because we needed a service mark. But no, we *wanted* people to use the term 'one-to-one' marketing and so we actively encouraged companies to do it. But I think both of us realized that people in companies were beginning to implement this and they were beginning to learn things about it and that if we really wanted to make a meaningful contribution in the field, then we had to get our hands dirty with real companies doing real things. We had to be kind of in the trenches. Right, Martha?

Martha: Yes, definitely. And people were saying: 'Can you help us? Can you answer some questions? Can you help us think this through?'

So you hadn't actually done consulting before?

Don: No, not really. Neither of us has a consulting background. We're not consultants. So when people say, 'Well, do you guys consult?' our answer's 'Sure, what do you want to know?'

Martha: 'We could give you some advice.'

Don: 'Yes, we'll give you some advice.' And occasionally somebody would hire one or the other or both of us to do one or two days a month of 'over the shoulder' coaching. But we decided we really needed to wade into this in more detail when we realized that if we weren't actually doing things for companies, the CRM revolution would not serve companies as well as we envisioned, and so we jumped in, both for field research and as a way to help companies.

That was the point at which we decided to get a venture capitalist to help underwrite the company, because we had to hire consultants, and we had to do consulting right. We couldn't just ladle out advice, but we had to hire people who really knew what they were doing in the area. We didn't really do any really serious consulting until 1999, and even then it wasn't very economically effective for us. I would say our first truly legitimate world-class consulting wasn't available until early 2001.

Do you do consulting yourselves?

Don: Primarily what we do is speaking engagements, and the truth is we are very expensive. So we incur a high opportunity cost when any single company engages us to do consulting . . .

Martha: . . . but it does happen. It would tend to work like this. I had an insurance company that paid the full rate for the day and I met with the 14 top people who report to the CEO in the morning and then made a speech to about 400 of the marketing and sales people, followed by a quick lunch meeting with some delivery people and so on. So it's a full day of working and demands a lot of preparation.

So they will hire you to come and do a talk, but you can also spend the day working with them in some cases?

Don: Often, yes. But it wouldn't be an engagement that lasted weeks. It's a day, sometimes two.

Martha: It would be unethical of us to suggest that the company needs us beyond that because it would be very, very expensive. Anyway, we have very smart people in the company who can do the type of consulting that companies need.

Don: A more frequent engagement for each of us would be to give a speech at some event where there might be an event sponsor. Say it's a computer company. As part of the event we give a talk to their user group and they may have three or four of their more important clients who would like to have one-on-one sessions with us. Whether those sessions are 45 minutes or two hours, those are very, very useful sessions and a lot of times they're basically free to the client company. As far as Martha and I are concerned, it's paid for in the speech. We like to be sure our speaking clients get all the added value we can afford to give them, but we also like to interact with a lot of different companies at a very high level. In addition to what we learn, it's actually a lot of fun.

Martha: And we also get an opportunity to go to universities where we can interact with students, or it might be an executive education program where the students are usually fairly senior people, so we get to hear their stories and solve their problems and work on those kinds of things. That's pretty exciting, too.

One more question before we leave the history. Who were the main influences, do you think, on your work?

Don: Was there any main influence on our work? Let me take a quick crack at that. I don't think there was any particular business thinker that was a bigger influence on our work than anybody else. We had this idea which was fairly original and it sort of came out of the air. However, we did admire a number of practitioners. We admired Charles Handy in the UK, for instance. He was the first person we quoted in *The One to One Future*. We admired his work. We liked Peter Drucker a lot as well. And we rate Regis McKenna very highly. He is a real groundbreaker.

Martha: And we were reading Fred Reichheld and Joe Pine. Actually, because I was in academia, I had the assignment of finding us a publisher for this book that we hadn't even outlined yet. And I naively called the publishers and they said, 'Have your agent call us. We don't want to talk to you, have your agent call.' So we knew we had to get an agent and then we realized well, if we're going to do this we may as well have an agent of a very good book, not just any old agent. So, we thought, 'Let's take the book that we really admire in this kind of space' and that was John Naisbitt's *Megatrends*. And the result is that we chose our agent, Rafe Sagalyn, because he was John Naisbitt's first agent. Rafe has been a valuable advisor for us.

Don: Then, when we set out to write the book, we had in mind a specific book that we wanted it to be like. That book was *Positioning: The Battle for Your Mind* by Al Ries and Jack Trout. I remember vividly when I was in the marketing department at an airline and I got my first job where I had to oversee advertising. I told my boss I didn't know anything about advertising. How could I do this?

But he said, 'Here, read this book', and he gave me *Positioning*. He said, 'Read this over the weekend and when you get done reading it the first time, read it again. When you've read it twice you'll know everything you need to know.'

Anyway, Martha and I wanted to have the same kind of impact for the relationship revolution as *Positioning* had for advertising, and frankly I think we succeeded. We're told that ours is the book people hand out to others when they say, 'What is this thing about relationships, what's going on?'

Current views of marketing

Let's move to the present. What is the current state of marketing?

Martha: I think that there's an interesting dichotomy, because a lot of people understand and believe that we have to have relationships with customers and we have to think about customer insight in order to do business. That's a very prevalent idea and it's kind of old news at this point. That's something that everybody gets. But, at the same time, I think very few companies have really been able to embrace true customer-centricity, in that they haven't really committed themselves to an understanding of one customer at a time, to using technologies to build the value of customers. They haven't gone beyond thinking about just the marketing campaign application.

What happened with *The One to One Future* was that we were getting more and more requests from clients to do something very fundamental, which is provide a business case justification for expenditures around this idea of customer relationships. Gosh, I'm going to have to spend money on technology, I'm going to have to spend money on consulting; I'm going to have to spend money on people. And then, if I'm the marketing director or the chief marketing officer (CMO), I'm going to have to go to my chief financial officer (CFO) to make the business case and they will work it in the way they always do and say, 'If you're asking for more money, prove that we're going to get a return on it.'

I think that there's an interesting dichotomy, because a lot of people understand and believe that we have to have relationships with customers and we have to think about customer insight in order to do business. That's a very prevalent idea and it's kind of old news at this point. That's something that everybody gets. But, at the same time, I think very few companies have really been able to embrace true customer-centricity.

Then we had this epiphany that, in fact, there was something even scarcer than the money that the CFO was holding in his or her little purse strings. And that was the number of customers, the actual customers, which that company was ever going to get. When we looked at it, it didn't make sense to us that companies would take so much care to budget the money they were investing, when what they were really limited by was the customers they had available to them. Shouldn't they think about maximizing the value those customers could create? And that's how our idea of return on the customer (ROC) came to us (*Return on Customer: Creating Maximum Value from Your Scarcest Resource*, 2005).

I will say that, from 1993 to 1997, we went through a change, in which we realized between *The One to One Future* and *Enterprise One to One* that this wasn't just a marketing story and it's not just a marketing issue. And we've pretty much stopped using the phrase 'one-to-one marketing'. People use it when they talk about us, but we don't really use the phrase anymore because we think the tasks a business has to undertake to develop and maintain a customer relationship go far beyond what most people consider 'marketing'.

Don: Marketing is too limiting.

Martha: Because it's only about the marketing department. But you really need to think about the whole enterprise. So we've moved further and further away from the restriction that what we're doing is about marketing, and we're moving closer and closer to the idea that what we're talking about is how to build shareholder value and assist the entire company in being all that it can be.

Don: So in our view, the future of marketing is that marketing is becoming everything in the company. Everything in the company is going to revolve around customer value: customers creating value for the business, which is, of course, the core purpose of any business.

What about financial analysts? Is there any sign that they are getting interested in this concept of return on customer?

Don: There is some. For example, Larry Kudlow of Kudlow and Company, the highly respected Wall Street commentator, endorsed the book and thinks it's really good. We're trying to get more attention from analysts, and the truth is that for most analysts this concept makes a lot of intuitive sense. The real issue is what kind of companies will disclose this information to analysts. Now, in the mobile phone category it's really easy. Every mobile phone company discloses its average revenue per user and its customer churn. With those two figures you can pretty much calculate the company's return on customer in any given year. You've got to fudge for customer base growth or shrinkage or whatever, but these are not substantial adjustments.

In other types of businesses, as companies get more sophisticated with their customer analytics, we expect investment analysts to ask them for this kind of data as well. We're actively trying to meet with groups of analysts in order to let them know what this metric is capable of doing.

Martha: Also, we've been trying to make the case that, if you are an investor, you'd like to know what ROC is. You really want to be able to detail the return on customer measures of different companies to make a decision. But, in addition to that, it will also drive better decisions in companies compared to what we've seen in the recent past, because the recent past has seen an embarrassment of short-term thinking that has really led us to a crisis. Recently I was moderating a panel of C-level officers address-ing the ROC issue, and the CFO of a large firm asked the audience to volunteer to help bring this ROC message to Wall Street.

Don: Yes, think about crises like Enron, WorldCom and Parmalat. All those crises are fundamentally rooted in the fact that managers who were overwhelmingly compensated for the short term had a great incentive to deceive shareholders and other stakeholders in order to enhance their own position.

Martha: If you can make yourself look good by making your short-term numbers look good, then you have a big incentive to do exactly that. But if, as ROC helps you do, you are being credited for your current revenues, while also being debited for how much future value you've had to give up to make those current numbers, then you may as well make the right de-cision right now, because you're going to pay for it either way.

And also you're very involved with the importance of issues of privacy and trust?

Don: We think that earning a customer's trust is literally the flipside of getting the customer to create the most value for you. Just think about your life as a consumer. If you have two, three or 20 different vendors to choose from, which is the one you're going to choose? Assuming that they all have more or less comparable products and services at comparable prices, you're going to choose the one with which you're most familiar or the one you trust the most.

When you follow this line of rea-soning to its conclusion, then you'll see that that if you can trust a company to always make recommen-dations to you that are in your inter-est, if you really trust the company to

> *We think that earning a customer's trust is literally the flipside of getting the customer to create the most value for you. Just think about your life as a consumer. If you have two, three or 20 different vendors to choose from, which is the one you're going to choose? Assuming that they all have more or less comparable products and services at comparable prices, you're going to choose the one with which you're most familiar or the one you trust the most.*

respect your interests, not just theirs, then you're going to want to do more business with the company, because every time you do business with them your own situation is improved; your interests are served.

So naturally there is a very, very strong correlation, and research has shown this, between what we call 'customer advocacy', which is advocating on the side of the customer – taking the customer's point of view – and the long-term financial success of a business. Now, all those elements of trust, such as taking a customer's point of view and advocating for the customer and treating a customer the way you'd like to be treated if you were the customer, necessarily imply that occasionally a company is going to have to give up some profit for itself in the short term in order to create longer-term loyalty.

The customer may call in to a company and be perfectly willing to buy a $1,000 financial services product when, in fact, your own expertise says that they don't really need to spend that much; they could get just as good a service by spending, say, $600. Well, there are two alternatives when you're faced with that. You could take the $1,000, realize that you've got an extra $400 more than you might have gotten and you're very profitable this quarter. Or you could say to the customer, 'You don't really need to spend $1,000; we could do this for $600.' Then you give up $400 in current value but you gain what is probably lifelong loyalty from the customer, plus recommendations from that customer to other customers.

It fits very easily with the whole employee culture, where you train your employees simply to watch out for customers' interests and always ask themselves, 'What's in the interest of the customer?' when they're solving a problem. It just makes a lot of sense and it's a very simple way for a company to adopt a philosophy that will tend to maximize their overall return on customers.

If it's so straightforward why do so few companies do this?

Don: Well, there are a lot of companies which will tell you the customer is king, the customer is always right, the customer is the boss and so forth. But for most of those, treating the customer the way you would treat yourself violates their short-term financial metrics, right? I don't want to give up that extra $400 that I could have gotten from the customer who's calling me and didn't know any better. I want that money and so the company looks at that and says, 'It would cost me something to give up that money. It would cost me $400.' As long as you're really focused on current results it's always going to be an unnatural act to treat the customer like you'd want to be treated.

But customers don't have just the short term in their own minds. Customers have memories, and they will change their future behaviours based on how you treat them in the present. How you treat car parts today has nothing at all to do with their cost to you in manufacturing more cars in the future. But how you treat a customer today has a great deal to do with how much value that customer creates for you in the future.

Doesn't it depend where the pressure on performance is coming from? Even if those at the top are interested in taking a longer-term view, what if those lower down want to go for the fast buck?

Don: We agree with that and we'll go one further. Even if this effort to earn customer trust is led from the top, if the investors haven't bought into it, sooner or later when you have a bad quarter the guy at the top is going to get his chain yanked. So that's why we started our first ROC book with an open letter to the financial community and we finish with a chapter to the CEO saying, 'Look, you cannot do this by yourself. You have to get your investors on board. Otherwise they won't let you get away with it.'

Martha: Which means that, right away, it's going to be an easier thing to accomplish and adopt for private companies, for smaller companies, for those who do not have public investors. Using Don's example, the problem right now is that you're getting rewarded for the $400 you keep this quarter. But you could also be penalized this quarter for the – let's think up a number – $5,000, say, that that customer would have spent if you'd treated him or her well this quarter but won't spend because he feels ripped off and doesn't want ever to do business with your company again. If you could be penalized today for losing that possible $5,000, then you probably would choose the $5,000 and build the value of your company instead of taking the quick $400.

Don: One more thing. What we have often said to people who question us about this issue of trust is that it's a time-honoured axiom in commerce that earning a customer's trust is the surest way to financial success. All we're doing is quantifying the benefit.

Martha: Right. We're proving that you can make money being a good guy. And, by the way, that doesn't mean that you can be a foolish guy. That doesn't mean that you treat your business as though it were a charity. Nor does it mean that cash doesn't matter. The role of discounting in cash flow must be used to calculate the relative cost of capital in any particular financial context.

That's not what we're suggesting. What we're suggesting is that you're always going to be better off by treating your customers and, for that matter, your partners and your suppliers and your employees fairly, than you will if you don't do those things.

Where is the marketer in all this? What do marketers need to do to be excellent to prosper in a modern environment?

Don: Well, today, I think that the frontier of marketing is in changing the culture of a company. It's a big frontier, but you want to create a trustworthy organization and one where employees all know that their single, primary mission is to earn and keep the trust of customers.

Does the impetus have to come from the top?

Martha: I think the idea that it's the CEO is very significant. Think about a company such as USAA Insurance. We dedicated one of our books to its former CEO, Brigadier-General Robert McDermott, because he built that business on a philosophy of building trust by taking the customer's point of view. He called it the company's Golden Rule of Customer Service: Treat the customer the way you would want to be treated if you were the customer.

So it does make sense that it's something that not just the marketing department will do, but that everybody will do who will ever touch a customer – which, by the way, is everybody, even though they don't literally touch customers every day. Imagine if we made every managerial decision all day, every day, based on whether or not we would increase the value of every one of our customers. If we did that, then it would drive trustworthy behaviour, it would drive smarter decisions, and it would balance short term and long term.

It's probably very easy to find companies that don't get it right.

Both: Very easy.

Are there ones that you've looked at and put your head in your hands, and thought: why?

Don: There are. We'd rather not talk about specific ones. I think there are obvious examples. When was the last time you dialled a company on the phone, got their voicemail and it said, 'Please enter your account number on the touch tone', so you did that. Then you were connected to a representative and what was the first thing you were asked? 'What's your account number?' OK? That's an example of a company that doesn't really care too much about its customers and the trust of its customers, doesn't look at itself from the customer's perspective.

Now, trust involves several different things. It involves reliability, it involves competence, it involves integrity, but it also involves self-orientation. That is, being customer-oriented means you are not self-oriented. Charles Green, one of the authors of the book *The Trusted Advisor* and whom we quote in our book, says that the willingness of a customer to trust a company is inversely proportional to the amount of self-orientation that the customer perceives on the company's part. In other words, the more I think that you're telling me something because you want to sell me something, the less I'm willing to trust you. So the opposite of self-orientation is . . .

Martha: Other-orientation.

Don: It's other-orientation. Treat the customer the way you'd like to be treated if you were the customer. Put yourself in the customer's shoes. Take the customer's point of view. No matter how you say it, it is a very simple, straightforward statement that is almost religious in its purity. It's a very basic idea that cuts through all the issues involved.

But it also goes against the traditional model of top-down management, doesn't it?

Don: Well, one of the things we suggest is that a company which really does this the right way will not only try to create this culture among its employees, but it will empower employees to solve problems within certain boundaries.

One example we gave was the ferry company Stena Line, operating in the Irish Sea, between Ireland and Great Britain. It reversed a terrible reputation for customer service by doing a number of different things to become customer-oriented, including better training and better employee management. And one of the innovations they introduced was something that Martha and I have often termed 'complaint discovery'. Within 30 minutes of disembarking, every passenger is intercepted by some crew member and asked whether everything went OK with their trip, 'Was there anything we should have done differently for you; do you have any problem with this cruise?' For anyone who has a problem, that crew member is authorized to spend up to £1,000 of Stena Line's money to fix it right then and there with no one's approval. They can do it immediately if they think it's required.

Now, in most cases, that involves something like half off on the next trip or an invite back or a companion ticket or something like that. And I doubt seriously that very many employees have actually found it necessary to spend the whole £1,000. But the very fact that they're allowed to means that no single employee at Stena anywhere can walk away from a customer problem saying, 'That's not my problem.' It *is* their problem. And that makes the organization extremely strong in its customer-orientation.

Isn't one of the problems that customers are just drowning in too much stuff?

Don: Oh, I think that's absolutely true. I think that people are overwhelmed and they're time short. They have very short attention spans and the marketers who really succeed are those who can help customers simplify their lives. And the greatest and easiest way to simplify those lives is to take on their burdens, solve their problems and gain their trust so that they give you more of their lives to handle. That's a perfect and highly demanded skill on the part of any company.

Getting more personal

Can we move to a more personal aspect? What do you think it was about the two of you as individuals that made you decide that these concepts were important enough to be disseminated to a wider audience?

Martha: Well, I was teaching creative subjects such as advertising, copywriting and layout to students who were then going out and trying to get jobs that were in shorter and shorter supply. Those jobs don't really exist the same way anymore and they were starting to disappear then. And I was feeling more and more like a fraud, that I was teaching them things that were less and less important.

I was watching the fragmentation of communication and thinking about what that meant for my students, for the kind of academic writing that I was required to engage in, in the 'publish or perish' academic environment. Then this idea came along and when we started having conversations about it and starting really thinking about it, I was so engrossed and excited about it that it would start waking me up at night to think about it.

I remember, early on in the first few speeches that I was asked to give, people would come up afterwards and they just had so many questions. There was a kind of thronging effect after the speeches because it was a real insight for people. So I guess what happened was that I wanted to do it despite what it meant for me professionally in academia. There I was, with a tenured position and I was told point blank 'You can write about this weird one-to-one stuff if you want to, Martha, but that won't count towards your promotion as full professor of marketing. Only your writing about traditional marketing and your research about traditional marketing is going to count.'

So I eventually did enough of that other stuff to get promoted to full professor, but this was what really mattered to me. I actually ended up changing departments within the university, from the marketing department to the telecommunications department, because it meant I could spend all my time teaching and writing about this rather than about the traditional 4Ps marketing. The people in this new department were all into the new communications technologies, and forward thinking about connections with people, about interactivity.

And I had a better time there, although it was a lateral move and I had the same salary, the same everything. But it was a more fun place to be. And then, of course, pretty soon the first book took off and I ended up resigning.

What about you, Don?

Don: Well, I've always had an entrepreneurial bug, even though I never took any business courses. I do vividly remember a formative experience. My first job when I got out of the air force was as an economist for an oil company. I was doing country studies and project studies and things like that and we had one situation where there was, I don't remember exactly what the controversy was, but there was some kind of controversy around some investment that I was being asked to evaluate. I was a little worried about the propriety of things and I remember having a conversation with my boss, who said that his boss, the president of the company, had three rules for being successful in business.

He said the rules were: make money, have fun, be ethical. And I've always remembered those three rules and for me one-to-one marketing and the books we've written, and now especially *Return on Customer*, have provided a tremendous opportunity to raise the ethical content of companies' customer-oriented activities. I would argue that the philosophies that we preach in *The One to One Future* and *Enterprise One to One* and so forth are fundamentally customer-friendly and customer-oriented. We are trying to make the world safe for customers.

> *I think that the philosophy that we talk about in* **Return on the Customer** *is based on the fact that the true 'killer app' in business success is earning the trust of customers. It's treating the customer the way you'd like to be treated if you were the customer. I would argue that that's got a strong, ethical and almost moral content to it. It gives me a great deal of satisfaction.*

And I think that the philosophy that we talk about in *Return on Customer* is based on the fact that the true 'killer app' in business success is earning the trust of customers. It's treating the customer the way you'd like to be treated if you were the customer. I would argue that that's got a strong, ethical and almost moral content to it. It gives me a great deal of satisfaction.

Martha: It's also a good thing I get to do professional speaking for a living because otherwise I would be accosting strangers on the street and saying: 'Let me save you from the future.' And I think that that is probably what it was. When Don and I had a chance to work together there was this realization that there were so many smart people who were kind of stuck in an era that was changing faster than they realized.

I compare it to the body image you have of yourself. It's hard for people who have lost weight or been through some major body change – it takes a while for their brains to catch up with the new body image. And I think that what we've seen is a lot of people who find it hard getting a new body image of what business is all about.

It's just very hard for people who are busy all day, every day, doing the jobs they have to do right now to keep their heads above water long enough to think: 'Where am I going, and where's my business going? What are my customers thinking about that they weren't thinking about before?' There are good, smart people trying to keep us in a healthy economy, and they usually don't have the luxury of being able to spend all their time looking at what's happening in business the way Don and I have been fortunate enough to do.

By the way, we adapted those three rules that Don learned early on to become the philosophy for Peppers & Rogers Group, which became: 'Have fun. Make money. Change the world.' That's the inside scoop. Publicly, our mission is to 'Help *customers* teach *companies* how to make money and grow.'

Martha, how would you describe Don?

Martha: Very energetic, very, very smart and fun to work with most of the time.

And Don, how would you describe Martha?

Don: I would describe Martha as a terrific brain that's just under the surface of a very dynamic personality.

Martha: Wow, thanks. Let me tell you about one of the things that I enjoy about working with Don. In academia you tend to work in groups. It's very unusual to have a solo effort because you have to pull in people with different expertise. And whenever I was working with anyone in academia I would hand over what I was supposed to do and then wait for weeks and then start bugging that person to get something back to me.

When I started working with Don I would do something, whatever my assignment was, flip it over to him and then go back to whatever else I had to do and, whoa, it was back already. And I loved the fact that I was not pulling and pulling and pulling trying to get things done, but rather running to keep up. It was great.

Did you have what you would consider a defining moment in your life – one that set you on the path you eventually followed?

Martha: The epiphany for me probably came from Don's speech, although we learned so much after that. In fact, nothing – not even the first book – has turned out the way we might have envisioned back when we first met. But I was game. I'd already started one business in graduate school which doubled my modest grad school income, and believed in figuring out and sharing the message even before we'd really had a chance to think it through.

Don: Not just one. I feel my entire life has been pointed toward what I'm doing right now, even though the truth is that my career choices and professional development have been determined much more by accident and happenstance than by premeditation. For instance, I have an undergraduate engineering degree, as well as a master's degree in international affairs, but I've never been an engineer or a diplomat.

My first job once I left the military, where I was an intelligence officer, was as an economist for an oil company. I then became the director of accounting for an airline. I also launched more than one of my own businesses during this time. They were all failures. I went into advertising only because it was a lot of fun and seemed pretty entrepreneurial. Once in the agency world, I gravitated to business development or 'new business', because it came naturally to me and because whenever I was involved in my own business I spent 95% of my time trying to win new clients.

What are you proudest of in terms of your work?

Don: The CRM revolution would have happened with or without Martha and me, of course. But I think it's safe to say that we hastened it into being and gave it a real life. We may not be the parents of CRM, per se, but it may be fair to say we're the midwives.

Personally, I've never liked to conform. I'm not really a rebel, but I do enjoy holding unpopular or perhaps revolutionary views, so the fact that our 'one-to-one marketing' idea was highly unconventional when we brought it out was very satisfying to me personally.

Martha: I would say I am proudest of our first one-to-one book, *The One to One Future*, and our first ROC book, *Return on Customer* (there will be more). Both books have been commercial successes, but what matters most is that they have influenced people's thinking. We often hear from people who say they've used these principles to create or grow a successful business. I think we have been very lucky to be in a position to help people out there who are researching and writing and doing a lot of good work and don't always get the attention they should. I'm also very proud that we have changed the way some people think about their 'business body image'.

We have been told that together we are more than the sum of the parts and that's sort of true. There have been times when one or the other of us has had a great opportunity to do something else and if we had been short-sighted we might have taken it up. Good for us that we didn't. I think our best work has been done together.

We have been told that together we are more than the sum of the parts and that's sort of true. There have been times when one or the other of us has had a great opportunity to do something else and if we had been short-sighted we might have taken it up. Good for us that we didn't. I think our best work has been done together.

Don: Hear, hear.

Selected publications

Return on Customer: Creating Maximum Value from Your Scarcest Resource, Currency Doubleday, 2005.

Managing Customer Relationships: A Strategic Framework, John Wiley & Sons, Inc. 2004.

One to One B2B: Customer Development Strategies for the Business-to-Business World, Currency Doubleday, 2001.

The One to One Manager: Real-World Lessons in Customer Relationship Management, Currency Doubleday, 1999.

The One to One Fieldbook: The Complete Toolkit for Implementing a 1to1 Marketing Program, Currency Doubleday, 1999. Co-author: Bob Dorf.

Enterprise One to One: Tools for Competing in the Interactive Age, Currency Doubleday, 1997.

The One to One Future: Building Relationships One Customer at a Time, Currency Doubleday, 1993.

6

John Quelch

Global marketing authority

John A. Quelch is Senior Associate Dean and Lincoln Filene Professor of Business Administration at Harvard Business School. Between 1998 and 2001 he was Dean of London Business School. Prior to 1998, he was the Sebastian S. Kresge Professor of Marketing and Co-Chair of the Marketing Area at Harvard Business School.

Quelch's research focus is on global marketing and branding in emerging as well as developed markets. He is the author, co-author or editor of 20 books, including The New Global Brands *(2006),* Global Marketing Management *(5th edition, 2005),* The Global Market *(2004),* Cases in Advertising and Promotion Management *(4th edition, 1996) and* The Marketing Challenge of Europe 1992 *(2nd edition, 1991). He has published articles on marketing issues in leading management journals such as* Harvard Business Review, McKinsey Quarterly *and* Sloan Management Review.

He is a nonexecutive director of WPP Group plc, Pepsi Bottling Group, Gentiva Health Services and Inverness Medical Innovations Inc. He also serves pro bono as Chairman of the Port Authority of Massachusetts and as a nonexecutive director of ACCION International, a leading microfinance lender. He has been a consultant, seminar leader and speaker for firms, industry associations and government agencies in more than 50 countries.

He was born in London, England, and was educated at Exeter College, Oxford University (BA and MA), the Wharton School of the University of Pennsylvania (MBA), the Harvard School of Public Health (MS) and Harvard Business School (DBA). In addition to the UK and USA, he has lived in Australia and Canada.

The professional journey

Let's go back to the beginning of your career. When did you leave the UK and why?

I went to the USA in 1972 to study for an MBA at Wharton, after I had read history at Oxford. Ironically, I was one of a few people who turned down a place at Harvard Business School to go to Wharton and I did that because I was really committed to a career in finance. I'd never really been exposed to marketing. In the UK 30 years ago marketing was essentially door-to-door encyclopaedia salesmen and didn't really have a tremendous cachet compared to finance. But what I discovered at Wharton was that marketing, especially with its focus on customer behaviour, the personal interactive aspect of it, the psychology, the buying processes and so on, interested me much more than the mathematics of corporate finance.

In 1974 I did make it to Harvard and studied for a doctorate there until 1977. Then I taught at the University of Western Ontario Business School, which is the principal business school in Canada, for two years and returned to Harvard Business School in 1979.

In your own words, what do you think you're best known for?

Probably two things: first, the early part of my career at Harvard Business School, until around 1985, was focused on below-the-line productivity improvement in sales promotion expenditures. And that was because 95 % of academic research into marketing communications concentrated on above-the-line advertising. Yet, when you looked at the numbers, about 60 % of total expenditures were on below-the-line activity. But hardly anyone was researching it.

I switched to a focus on global marketing around 1985. Again, that was long before global marketing or globalization became fashionable. The Berlin Wall fell in 1989 and, as a result, globalization became much more important. And the opening up of China, India and many other world economies – plus the former Soviet Union – really fuelled a lot of interest in international market expansion by Western multinationals during the 1990s. I was fortunately well-placed to ride that wave.

I switched to a focus on global marketing around 1985. Again, that was long before global marketing or globalization became fashionable. The Berlin Wall fell in 1989 and, as a result, globalization became much more important. And the opening up of China, India and many other world economies – plus the former Soviet Union – really fuelled a lot of interest in international market expansion by Western multinationals during the 1990s. I was fortunately well-placed to ride that wave.

Do you think that part of the interest arose from the fact that you came from the other side of the Atlantic, as it were?

Not particularly. It was really because my father was in the Royal Air Force and we had been posted around the world when I was growing up. Many internationalists are children of diplomats or military personnel who've had those childhood experiences. Or they're sons or daughters of people who've worked in multinational companies and lived overseas.

When you're being transferred from one location to another you have to be very quick to adapt to new environments, quick to understand how to fit in. You have to develop a sensitivity to and curiosity about your environment and to the way people are behaving and what they expect. That enables you to be adaptive. It becomes a very good recipe for managing in an international cross-cultural context.

What or who were the main influences on your work in the early days?

I think the people who influenced me the most early on were other academics. One was Yoram (Jerry) Wind. He is now a senior professor at Wharton. At the time I attended Wharton, he was an associate professor with a terrific course on new product development: half of the course sessions were lectures but the other half involved doing a new product development project in a team. Jerry was a great coach and a hugely enthusiastic yet demanding instructor.

When I read today about the importance of getting more action learning into the classroom and more team development and so on, all this was encapsulated in the course that I took from him in 1973.

The second person was another Wharton professor, Leonard Lodish. He is really a marketing science wiz, a very good modeller. What fascinated me about him was that he taught a course on advertising in which you never saw an ad – something which I thought was simultaneously brilliant and ridiculous.

Isn't that a somewhat unusual approach for a course in advertising?

Yes, but he was so into the quantification of advertising's impact on sales and modelling it, that he had little interest in the fuzzy creative aspects of advertising. It was really incredible. Advertising is a subject that will attract a lot of students who think they're going to have an easy time taking a gut course. Lodish wanted to do exactly the opposite and give them a real challenge – which he did.

But what was it about it that got your interest?

First, it was such a surprising approach to teaching the subject. Second, it was the idea that something as seemingly subjective could be amenable to rigorous scientific analysis. That was its attraction.

Had you had any experience of advertising?

That's a good question. I suppose I can look back to my stint as the editor of the Oxford University newspaper, *Cherwell*, in 1971. *Cherwell* was and still is a free-standing paper that has no economic subsidy from the university. It exists financially on the basis of sales and advertising revenues from each weekly issue. That was a genuine and exciting business management experience at the age of 19, from which you could say I never recovered.

Prior to being the editor, I'd been the business manager, so I'd had to use some foot leather to visit retailers and restaurants in Oxford to solicit advertising for the paper. I remember being slightly ashamed about managing to persuade this wonderful storeowner on the Cowley Road, who had a small apparel store, that it would be great for him to advertise on the front page of the *Cherwell* and to provide a special discount coupon offer in his advertisements – for Levi's, if I remember rightly, a product of obvious relevance to students.

When we went back to him, a month after these ads had run, he reported that not a single coupon had been redeemed. I felt bad that we had taken money from an honest retailer to promote his store when, in reality, the location of his store was so out of the way from where any student would be cycling by that it would be ridiculous to expect them to be drawn to it. Should we have refunded the cost of the advertisements? I still don't know. We didn't.

When you began to talk about globalization and marketing, did you actually use the term 'international' as opposed to 'globalization'?

In 1983 Ted Levitt published a famous *Harvard Business Review* article, 'The Globalization of Markets'. I was in a slightly difficult position because I had been hired by Levitt at Harvard, but I didn't agree with his thesis. So I co-authored an article for the *Harvard Business Review* called 'Customizing Global Marketing', which took him on – in the nicest possible way, since I was not tenured at the time. The importance of this is that it relates to your question. It was not customizing *international* marketing, but customizing *global* marketing. The one thing that Levitt did was launch the word 'global', whereas previously people had only used the words 'international' or 'multinational'.

Did you see a difference? A shading in definition?

Yes. The word 'international' implies that the nation is the core unit of analysis. You're talking about things that happen between nations. The word 'multinational' still views the nation as the starting point. The word 'global' obviously takes a wholly different perspective.

What were the sorts of challenges you faced when you began to write about this?

Because I was arguing the case for local adaptation contingent on market circumstances and product category characteristics, I didn't have to take the kind of criticism that Levitt took. He was a brilliant provocateur and word-smith, and delighted in the provocation he created. But when it came to addressing the issue what one discovers is that, depending upon the product category and the size and strategic importance of the country in question, you can have arguments for different levels of adaptation or standardization.

My contribution, I think, was to provide some contextual guidance to enable managers to figure out in what market circumstances and for what product categories to push globalization and how far to push it through the marketing mix. The 1986 article includes two planning matrixes which are still used by many companies. They can use them to have a dialogue within the corporation about how much adaptation or standardization to apply to elements of the marketing mix, for which products and in which country markets.

Have you found that the idea of adaptation has been more straightforward for companies better used to dealing with different cultures – European versus American, for example?

Not as much as you would think. For instance, my 1986 article spends quite a lot of time contrasting Nestlé with Coca-Cola. Nestlé is, of course, a much more decentralized multinational that focuses on keeping lines of responsibility clearly associated with the individual country manager. That makes perfect sense for the food products business, which is obviously much more culturally sensitive than high technology, for example.

With Coca-Cola, part of the value proposition was that you bought a piece of Americana, so a more global standardized approach was much more appropriate. And although Coca-Cola is a beverage and therefore you might say. 'Well, it's pretty similar to food', in actuality most Coca-Cola is consumed outside the home. Second, it's always drunk on its own – in other words, you don't mix Coca-Cola on your plate with mashed potatoes and gravy, right? So as a result of those two characteristics it can be marketed much more easily with a standard global proposition. And its very 'globalness', the fact that everybody around the world is consuming it, is actually a major selling point.

That's why you'll find Coca-Cola being sold 1,000 miles up the Amazon. The people in that village really value the fact that once every three weeks, or whenever they can afford a can of it, they become part of a global village that's way beyond their mundane daily life. So although that may sound a little bit hokey to you and me, Coke's very globalness is a major part of the value proposition of this brand.

You've been teaching for a long time. What do you enjoy about it?

I enjoy case study teaching because of the human interaction and the unpredictability of each class. The same case can generate quite different student discussions, if one is sufficiently flexible and confident to let students set the direction. Recently I was teaching the Starbucks case that I wrote with Youngme Moon a couple of years ago. I've probably taught it about 10 times so far, but there were two or three fascinating points that came up in this class discussion that I hadn't heard or thought of before. Interactive case teaching is vastly more interesting to me than giving the same lecture for the tenth time.

Had you ever considered working in industry?

I went straight from Oxford to Wharton so I have never worked full-time outside of academia. Many people share the prejudice that, if you have not worked outside of academia, you must be a complete egghead.

What I've discovered is that many of the people who have worked outside academia and then come back into it are people who didn't enjoy the real world and fled back into the monastery and are often quite impractical. On the other hand, those of us who have never worked outside of academia have, in many cases, striven to fight the prejudice by engaging in practical business activity – not least of which is being on the boards of major companies to make sure that we remain relevant in our thinking.

And do you do a lot of consulting?

Yes, but I don't do as much as I used to do because I found that I have a particular skill as a non-executive director. I have a tremendous amount of nonexecutive director experience, having served on the boards of 10 public companies on both sides of the Atlantic. The key is to support the chief executive officer (CEO) and his or her team to ensure that they are as successful as they possibly can be in adding value to the shareholders.

One of these companies being, of course, WPP. Is that a fascinating company to see at such close hand?

Yes, I joined the WPP board 18 years ago so I've had the privilege of an inside view of a company (and a businessman) that has changed the face of an industry. What's not understood sufficiently about Sir Martin Sorrell is the degree to which he has reinvented the advertising and marketing services industry – and as a marketer, not as a financier – though he will always be admired for bringing financial discipline to advertising.

First, he saw in the late 1970s the importance of below-the-line promotion (versus above-the-line advertising). When he left Saatchi & Saatchi, he set up an agency that was intended to focus just on below-the-line activity. But his vision was flexible. When the opportunity arose to acquire the J. Walter Thompson company, he understood that what was needed by most clients was an integrated solution that included both above-the-line and below-the-line components.

Second, Martin understood the potential for media buying to become a major source of expertise and profit in the marketing services world. As recently as 10 years ago, the media departments of most advertising agencies were regarded as backwaters and were often staffed with second-tier personnel.

Today the media buying agencies, which are separate brands from the creative agencies, have become a very important force for revenue and profit generation within the marketing services holding companies. Martin is someone who not only understands but shapes the industry and is ahead of the curve on many upcoming trends.

Current views of marketing

Can any brand be global, in your view?

High technology companies are supranational in the sense that the technology itself is universal. It's easier for American technology companies to present themselves as supranational brands than it is for food manufacturers because food is so much more culture-bound.

The best historical example in this regard is IBM. Thomas Watson committed IBM to support local communities wherever it happened to operate, whether France, Germany or the United States. This wasn't because IBM wanted to adapt to the market – adaptation costs money – but because IBM wanted its people to be close to the communities that they served and to be seen as a good local citizen.

The challenge is greatest for the companies which champion the more culturally-bound or iconic brands. That would include Disney, Coca-Cola and McDonald's. These are brands with an obvious American heritage; to deny or downplay it would be unauthentic and probably deplete rather than add to the strength of the brand.

Wherever you go in the world, there is a certain minority percentage of consumers who are either anti-global, and will go out of their way to avoid global brands, or they're anti-American and will go out of their way to avoid American brands.

But our research suggests most consumers don't let foreign policy perceptions affect their purchase behaviours. You can see this most clearly in the case of the various knock-offs of Pepsi-Cola and Coca-Cola that sprang up in Muslim countries during the Iraq war: Mecca Cola, for example. They gained some short-term traction but it wasn't long before consumers returned to their preferred global brands.

If you look at Pepsi-Cola sales in Arab countries, I think it's fair to say that they have increased over pre-Iraq war levels in almost every market.

I'm pretty sceptical about attempted consumer boycotts of American brands having that much of a sales impact.

However, where you have brands for which there are high quality, local or non-American substitutes, the global brands will clearly be more vulnerable than those that have built up a strong differentiated identity and brand equity.

Where are we with globalization at the moment? Do most companies understand it?

There is an understanding of the pros and the cons of globalization and that the pros dramatically outweigh the cons. But there is something else that's very important: a tremendous increase in commitment – especially among European multinational corporations – to corporate social responsibility (CSR) at a level that 20 years ago you would never have seen.

Doug Holt and I found that in research which we published in the *Harvard Business Review* in September 2004, called 'How Global Brands Compete'. One of our findings, which we hadn't expected, was the significance of consumer perceptions of corporate social responsibility as a factor in determining brand preferences. Consumers may be willing to pay a premium for a global brand, but they also expect a much higher level of CSR from that global brand than they would expect from an equivalent local brand.

We also found that, in many emerging markets, there is a strong support for global brands as vehicles for bringing better practices into the management of labour forces and better quality control systems, which then raise standards for everybody in those economies. This is one reason you don't hear national governments in emerging economies complaining about global corporations. The best are a strong positive force for economic development. The criticism of global cor-

> *There is an understanding of the pros and the cons of globalization and that the pros dramatically outweigh the cons. But there is something else that's very important: a tremendous increase in commitment – especially among European multinational corporations – to corporate social responsibility at a level that 20 years ago you would never have seen.*

porations typically comes from nongovernmental organizations (NGOs) and activist groups.

You could argue that governments are so dependent on foreign direct investment that they can't oppose global companies. But another, strong explanation is that the global corporations really do help these national governments set new standards and expectations for the performance of local companies.

To what extent should companies engage with NGOs?

Like anything else in life, not all NGOs are created equal. There are some NGOs that are hostile to business and to the capitalist system and it's probably of little use trying to engage with them. But there are many NGOs that view business as highly resourced and highly skilled and as capable of adding tremendous value if they can be persuaded to partner in solving social problems. The World Wildlife Federation, now known as WWF, is one such example.

Why?

It has an excellent track record of partnering with business. One motive is, of course, to obtain funding from business for the work of the WWF. Second, collaborative or joint communications enhance exposure for WWF, while at the same time the partner company in question is presumably getting some kudos from being 'endorsed' by the NGO. Third, and most important, WWF will partner with companies only if there is a big conservation component to the agreement, whereby the company agrees to certain targets that it wouldn't otherwise have agreed to, as well as independent monitoring of its performance against those targets. WWF is an NGO that's constructively engaging with the corporate sector to achieve its goals, rather than simply making a lot of noise.

Turning to marketing specifically, what do you see as the biggest challenges facing marketing professionals?

The biggest challenge is to document the return on investment of marketing expenditures. Many other functional areas of the corporation, such as manufacturing and logistics, have been subjected to progressively more rigorous quantitative analysis and cost reduction programming. But marketing still has not seen sufficient scientific rigour applied to its expenditures for CEOs and non-marketing people to have confidence that the money they invest in marketing is truly not, to paraphrase John Wanamaker, the half that's being wasted.

Is the problem the people attracted to marketing in the first place?

Yes, I think it's partly that there's a resistance among marketers to submit themselves to process analysis and process improvement. People who are attracted to marketing tend to enjoy and thrive on ambiguity. In other words, they're usually very good communicators, but not necessarily enthusiastic about being held accountable for the achievement of particular performance metrics.

What you need to have in marketing is a combination of right-brain and left-brain thinking. You need the creativity and the imagination, but you also need the rigour and discipline that will convince non-marketing people at board level to continue to invest money in marketing. You don't often find great left- and right-brain skills in a single person, but across any marketing department you need a combination of left-brain thinkers and right-brain thinkers, and processes to enable them to work together.

In an article for the *Wall Street Journal* in 2005, I called this combination of creative flair and financial discipline 'ambidextrous marketing'. I included this quote from Procter & Gamble's (P&G) chief marketing officer: 'Marketing is a $450 million industry, and we are making decisions with less data and discipline than we apply to $100,000 decisions in other aspects of our business.'

But even a left-brain, more analytical person in marketing still needs an appreciation of, and a respect for, the end consumer. So in assessing someone's suitability for a career in marketing, quite frankly, I still try to size up whether they genuinely like people and are curious about them.

Which companies do you rate highly, particularly in terms of your areas of expertise?

One is Nestlé, for two reasons. Number one is its consistent appreciation that people in every market are still different and that, if you want to penetrate deeper into a national market in a particular product category, you have to offer progressively more and adapted products. You can't expect to conquer the entire market with a single product. You can skim the surface of every country market with some globally standardized premium-positioned product, but you can't drill deep into the market without investing in local adaptation.

Second, Nestlé still retains the simple, elegant delegation of profit-and-loss responsibility to a single country manager in each market. In doing that, the company sacrifices something in terms of operational efficiency, but it is administratively very clear and accountability cannot be ducked. There is no room for the finger pointing that can characterize a matrix type of organization.

Next, I would have to mention P&G. Under chairman and CEO A.G. Lafley, the company has rediscovered the basics of customer understanding as its core competence. P&G is relentlessly committed to understanding the customer better than anyone else. Fundamentally, that's what good marketing has to be based upon. But, so often, in the race to deliver quarterly results for Wall Street, there's a lot more emphasis on just coming out with new products and seeing what sticks as opposed to really understanding consumers and identifying latent needs that maybe are not expressed in consumer research, but are the core unmet needs that breakthrough new products should be addressing.

Then there is Harrah's, the casino operator. It was an also-ran in an industry where it could not compete with major casino operators like Steve Wynn and Donald Trump on their terms. Harrah's simply didn't have the money to build the next Bellagio in Las Vegas, the next $100-million casino with blockbuster entertainment and spectacular public spaces.

So what Harrah's CEO, Gary Loveman, did was focus on something that the others weren't focusing on – customer intimacy – and develop the best customer relationship management system and the technology associated with it in the world. Harrah's can very economically tailor offerings to each customer no matter how little they're spending with the casino by predicting future potential based on their observed behaviour. In this example, marketing science and left-brain marketing allow for customized offerings to consumers who are not spending much money and who would therefore be ignored by most other casino operators.

Are there any companies which are obviously getting it wrong?

I think Kraft is a really sad story. It used to be a phenomenal brand. But it has been allowed to deteriorate as a result of stop/go investment in marketing. Those who've been running it have periodically invested heavily in marketing and then, when that investment has not immediately paid back, they have voluntarily or been forced to cut it back. If you are operating a stop/go approach towards brand franchise building, you cannot expect good results over the long term.

Finally, do you think marketing is held in higher esteem in the USA than in Europe?

I think the gap is less than it used to be. When I left England in 1972 to do my MBA at Wharton, I had no concept of marketing as being a subject that one would study seriously, let alone be the focus of a lifetime career.

Getting more personal

What do you think it is about you as a person that attracted you to these concepts and ideas?

In academia, just as on a supermarket shelf, a professor is a product competing for shelf space and he or she has to be positioned properly in a persuasive fashion. Obviously, with my international background, I was a credible and confident researcher in this particular arena. Quite frankly, one thing led to the other. Without the childhood experience and without being a non-American in America, it would have been harder to have had the insights to carve out this particular territory.

What are you proudest of?

That over the course of 30 years I have written approximately 300 case studies and teaching notes. There is hardly anyone who takes a marketing course in an MBA program in the world who doesn't have something that I've written in his or her curriculum.

That impact in the classroom is as important to me as ideas generated in the research. Though one of the important things to understand is that, in the Harvard Business School model, the research feeds off the teaching and the case writing is often part and parcel of a professor's research program.

Over the course of 30 years I have written approximately 300 case studies and teaching notes. There is hardly anyone who takes a marketing course in an MBA program in the world who doesn't have something that I've written in his or her curriculum.

When I was doing my early research on sales promotion, there was not much on it in the serious marketing literature, so my approach to research was to go out and study sales promotion in 10 companies, write 10 case studies and then draw some generalizations out of that collective research, rather than go into a laboratory and try to model something that I had no understanding of.

Do you have what you can see now was a defining moment in your life?

Well, just for fun I'll give you one that is not really a defining moment but it's a good story. When my family was posted to Australia in 1957 I was six years old. It then took two and a half days to travel from London to Sydney by air. We flew Qantas on a Super Constellation aircraft. It was a four-propeller plane with three vertical tailfins and quite distinctive looking.

We stopped in Paris, Frankfurt, Rome, Athens, Beirut, Baghdad, Karachi, Calcutta, Singapore, Darwin and then Sydney. So it was like doing the Jules Verne book *Around the World in 80 Days* in two days instead of 80. Given I was only six years old, I remember a tremendous number of experiences along the way. But the strongest memory is when we landed in Darwin, Australia, at about 7 a.m.

Darwin Airport in 1957 basically comprised a runway and one shack, but we went in to get breakfast while the plane was refuelled. I remember looking at the breakfast menu and being amazed to see steak and chips listed. So the first meal that I had in Australia as a six-year-old was steak and chips in Darwin Airport and I remember saying to my father: 'Dad, I'm really glad we came to this country. This is terrific.'

Selected publications

The New Global Brands: Managing Non-Governmental Organizations in the 21st Century, Southwestern Publishing Company, 2006. Co-author: Nathalie Laidler-Kylander.

Global Marketing Management, Southwestern Publishing Company, 2005, 5th edn. Co-author: Christopher A. Bartlett.

Marketing Management, McGraw-Hill, 2005. Co-authors: R. Lal and V.K. Rangan.

Problems and Cases in Health Care Marketing, McGraw-Hill Irwin, 2005. Co-authors: John T. Gourville and V. Kasturi Rangan.

The Global Market: Developing a Strategy to Manage Across Borders, Jossey-Bass, 2004. Co-author: Rohit Deshpandé.

Cases in Strategic Marketing Management: Business Strategies in Muslim Countries, Prentice-Hall, 2001.

Cases in Strategic Marketing Management: Business Strategies in Latin America, Prentice-Hall, Inc., 2001. Co-author: G. D'Andrea.

Cases in Marketing Management and Strategy: An Asia Pacific Perspective, Prentice-Hall Asia, 1996. Co-authors: Siew Meng Leong, Swee Hoon Ang and Chin Tiong Tan.

Cases in Product Management, Richard D. Irwin, Inc., 1995.

Cases in Advertising and Promotion Management, Richard D. Irwin, Inc., 1994, 4th edn. Co-author: P. Farris.

Cases in European Marketing Management, Richard D. Irwin, Inc., 1994. Co-authors: Kamran Kashani and S. Vandermerwe.

Global Marketing Management, Addison-Wesley, 1994, 3rd edn. Co-authors: Robert D. Buzzell and Christopher A. Bartlett.

Marketing Management, Richard D. Irwin Inc., 1993. Co-authors: R.J. Dolan and T. Kosnik.

Ethics in Marketing, Richard D. Irwin, Inc., 1992. Co-author: N.C. Smith.

Cases in Advertising and Promotion Management, Richard D. Irwin, Inc., 1991, 3rd edn. Co-author: P. Farris.

Global Marketing Management, Addison-Wesley, 1991, 2nd edn. Co-authors: Robert D. Buzzell and Christopher A. Bartlett.

The Marketing Challenge of Europe 1992, Addison-Wesley, 1990. Co-authors: Robert D. Buzzell and E. Salama. 2nd edn 1991. French, Italian, Japanese, Spanish translations, 1992.

How to Market to Consumers: Ten Ways to Win, John Wiley & Sons, Inc., 1989.

Sales Promotion Management, Prentice-Hall, 1989. Japanese translation, 1991.

Multinational Marketing Management, Addison-Wesley, 1988. Co-author: R. Buzzell. 2nd edn, *Global Marketing Management*, with R. Buzzell and C. Bartlett, 1992. 3rd edn, *Global Marketing Management*, with R. Buzzell and C. Bartlett, 1995. 4th edn, *Global Marketing Management*, with C. Bartlett, 1999.

Trade Promotion and Food Distribution Costs, Food Marketing Institute, 1987. Monograph. Co-authors: R. Buzzell and W. Salmon.

Cases in Consumer Behavior, Prentice-Hall, 1986. 2nd edn. Co-authors: F.S. Debruicker and S. Ward.

Marketing Management: Principles, Analysis and Applications, Richard D. Irwin, Inc., 1985. Co-authors: B.P. Shapiro and R.J. Dolan.

Marketing Management: Readings from Theory to Practice. Richard D. Irwin, Inc., 1985. Co-authors: B.P. Shapiro and R.J. Dolan.

Marketing Management: Strategy, Planning and Implementation, Richard D. Irwin, Inc., 1985. Co-authors: B.P. Shapiro and R.J. Dolan.

Advertising and Promotion Management. Chilton Book Company, 1983. Co-author: P. Farris. 2nd edition, Krieger Publishing Company, 1987.

Cases in Advertising and Promotion Management. Business Publications, Inc., 1983. Co-author: P. Farris. 2nd edn, 1987. 3rd edn, Richard D. Irwin, Inc., 1991. 4th edn, Richard D. Irwin, Inc., 1994.

Marketing Communications in a Changing Environment. 1983. Edited compilation of *Harvard Business Review* articles, No. 14081, Monograph.

John Quelch has also written numerous articles in various academic and professional journals.

7

....

Al Ries

Pioneer of positioning

Al Ries is chairman of Ries & Ries, an Atlanta-based marketing strategy firm. He is a legendary marketing strategist and the bestselling author (or co-author) of 11 books on marketing including Positioning: The Battle for Your Mind, Marketing Warfare, Focus, The 22 Immutable Laws of Branding, The Fall of Advertising and the Rise of PR *and his latest,* The Origin of Brands.

After graduating from DePauw University, he worked in the advertising department of General Electric (GE) before founding his own advertising agency in New York City, Ries Cappiello Colwell. The agency later changed to a marketing strategy firm, Trout & Ries.

In 1994, he started Ries & Ries with his daughter Laura. They continue to work together consulting with Fortune 500 companies, writing books and giving seminars around the world.

He was president of the Association of Industrial Advertisers (now the Business Marketing Association) and the Advertising Club of New York. He was also chairman of the Club's Andy Awards. In 1989, Sales and Marketing Executives International gave him its 'Tops in Marketing' award. In 1999, PR Week magazine named him one of the 100 most influential PR people of the 20th century.

His book, The Fall of Advertising and the Rise of PR, *has generated enormous interest in the marketing community. The book made both the* Business Week *and the* Wall Street Journal *bestseller lists. In addition to being reviewed by these publications, it was also reviewed by* USA Today, Harvard Business Review, Boston Globe, Chicago Sun-Times *and many other publications.*

His latest release, The Origin of Brands, *explores 'divergence', the best way to create a new brand. The concept is analogous to the creation of a new species, as pioneered by Charles Darwin in his classic book on the subject. He writes a monthly marketing column for AdAge.com and is an often-quoted expert in many publications.*

The professional journey

What, in your view, are you best known for?

Two things – positioning and focus. And they complement one another.

Back in the 1950s and 1960s, advertising was considered a form of communication. You communicated the features and benefits of the product or service being advertised. Even today, some people refer to advertising as 'marketing communications'. We wondered, however, why some ad campaigns worked and others didn't. How could two campaigns display little difference in their communications value yet enormous differences in their effectiveness?

Perhaps, we speculated, the differences were in the prospects' minds. We noted that, when advertising campaigns were directed at an 'open mind', they were usually effective. When directed at 'closed minds', they were usually ineffective.

In other words, when somebody else owned the 'position' in the mind, you couldn't convince the prospect that your product or service was better, no matter whether the facts were on your side or not.

Could you give a few examples?

Both RCA and GE failed in their attempts to launch a line of mainframe computers. What should they have done? RCA was perceived as a leader in communications, so it should have introduced a 'communications' computer. GE was perceived as a leader in time-sharing, so it should have introduced a 'time-sharing' computer.

Eventually this thinking led to a complete reversal of the normal way of doing things. Instead of concentrating on the 'sending' side, we reversed the order and concentrated on the 'receiving' side. The first thing to do was to look into the mind of the prospect and decide what 'positions' were available. Then tailor the message to one of these open positions. Sometimes, this requires a change of product, a change of the product's features, or even a change of the product's name.

Advertising Age magazine, the advertising industry's 'bible', selected positioning as one of the 75 most important moments in advertising in the last 75 years. This, along with the unique selling proposition, motivational research and copy testing, were the only four conceptual ideas selected by the publication.

Basically, it's a technique for preparing a communications program. It does not, however, tell you how to find an open position in the prospect's mind. That's where 'focus' comes in.

Would you give some examples of 'focus'?

It's always possible to find an open position by 'narrowing the focus'. For example, Emery Air Freight was the leading air cargo carrier. So Federal

Express narrowed its focus to 'overnight' air cargo and thus became market leader. Subway narrowed its focus to 'submarine sandwiches' and evolved into the fifth largest fast-food chain in America. Pepsi-Cola wanted to compete with market leader Coca-Cola. It narrowed its focus to 'younger' people (the Pepsi Generation). Today, Pepsi is a strong number two brand.

I took these ideas and used them in a book, *Focus: The Future of Your Company Depends on It.*

What do you think makes focus such a powerful concept?

It goes against logical thinking. Many marketing and management people assume that the broader the line, the better. The more market segments that a brand can appeal to, the greater the sales. It's logical, but it doesn't work that way.

It's not a sales but a brand problem. The broader the line, the more segments you try to appeal to, the weaker the brand. If you try to stand for everything, you stand for nothing. What's a Chevrolet? It's a large, small, cheap expensive car or truck and a very weak brand.

Also, many marketing and management people assume that a narrowly focused brand will automatically have small sales. Not necessarily, because they don't consider the mind of the prospect. Take Volvo, for example, a brand focused on safety. By narrowing its focus, Volvo was able to achieve great credibility for the brand. Here's where psychology comes in. It's called the 'halo effect'. A good-looking person, for example, is assumed to have a lot of other favourable qualities.

If Volvo is good at safety, it must be good at making dependable, high quality cars with good gas mileage and many other favourable attributes. It may not necessarily be true, but that's the general perception.

Focus goes against logical thinking. Many marketing and management people assume that the broader the line, the better. The more market segments that a brand can appeal to, the greater the sales. It's logical, but it doesn't work that way. It's not a sales but a brand problem. The broader the line, the more segments you try to appeal to, the weaker the brand. If you try to stand for everything, you stand for nothing.

Let's look at your history. You joined GE in 1950. What had you done before and why did you join the ad department?

That was my first job. And I'd wanted to get into advertising since I read a book about advertising by Frederic Wakeman called *The Hucksters*. It sounded like an exciting business, so I wanted to get into it.

You've said, in the past, that you waited nine years to write your first book on positioning with Jack Trout and you wish you hadn't. So why the wait?

The timing of a book is very important. A book can be a big hit one year if the timing is right and we had made a big, big impact with the *Advertising Age* series in 1972. In fact, the reason it took nine years is because we were so busy due to its success. I was making speeches, handling new business, running around the country and doing all sorts of stuff.

That's why we missed the bigger opportunity, which was to come out with a book. The difference between a book and magazine articles is that articles can make a big, big impact in a short period of time – the month they come out – but a year or so later it's gone. A book like Darwin's *Origin of the Species*, by contrast, which came out in 1859, would have disappeared if it had been just a magazine article. So the articles had a big impact, but it didn't last like the book. Our book, *Positioning: The Battle for Your Mind*, wasn't published until 1981.

How did you promote positioning?

I don't think I ever consciously made the decision to promote positioning, or other concepts, to a wider audience. Most of my books, magazine articles and other forms of communications were undertaken as the result of specific requests. It was Bill Sabin, an editor at McGraw-Hill, for example, who suggested that *Positioning* would make a good book. He then nagged us until we wrote it.

It was the encouragement and support of other people that led me to become an author and a speaker but, with hindsight, I reckon that younger people generally just don't think about writing books.

How did it evolve into such a firm concept?

Our experience in advertising made the idea so powerful for us. By 1972, I'd spent 22 years in advertising. What I found, though, was that very little communication takes place. It's funny. People can tell you Rolex is the best watch, Heinz is the best ketchup – but when you ask them what they know about an automobile, a watch or anything else they know very, very little.

Take Rolex. Most people say, 'Well, it's the best watch', yet they can't tell you anything about its manufacture. Or they know it's made in Switzerland, but nothing about the product. And that's true with many brands. While the advertising might be loaded with facts and information, very little of that gets communicated to the prospect. We realized that the entire industry is just focused on entirely the wrong idea, the idea being you communicate. But how can you communicate if very little communication takes place?

So the flip side is, when there's an open hole in the mind, when you're first in a new category, a new brand instantly fills that hole. But if you try to compete, as we mentioned in the 1972 articles, against, say, IBM in mainframe computers, it's very, very difficult. And yet during that period – the 1960s and 1970s – a lot of big companies, including GE, ran massive advertising campaigns talking about their mainframe computer lines and all the benefits.

You were shaking up traditional notions of advertising?

These are big issues, which led to the thinking behind *The Fall of Advertising and the Rise of PR*, where we (myself and my daughter Laura) talk about the biggest problem: lack of credibility hampering advertising's ability to communicate.

People don't believe a message sent by an advertiser on the basis that, hey, that's self-interest at work. But they do believe a message when they read it in a magazine or newspaper. That's a third party, that's independent, that's not connected with the advertiser, so that has credibility. So these issues of credibility and communications became the two biggest issues.

You could say, 'Why do advertising at all?' Well, in the long run we believe that advertising is like cheerleading. You get out there, repeat ideas that already exist in the mind and reinforce them. The role and function of advertising today, at least in our opinion, is to transform people's weak opinions about a brand into strong ones without changing their minds.

Was working at GE seminal for your thinking?

Until you can personally experience the effect of advertising on a company's sales, you cannot become a good advertising strategist. The 'how' is harder. One of the first things I did at General Electric was subscribe to *Advertising Age*. That means I've been a reader of the advertising business's 'bible' for more than 50 years.

It carried many articles about and by such advertising legends as Bill Bernbach, David Ogilvy and many others. I always read them very carefully.

Over the years, I have broadened my reading to include dozens of magazines and newspapers including *The Wall Street Journal*, *The New York Times*, *USA Today*, *Business Week*, *Fortune*, *Forbes* and many others. If you want to be a marketing expert, you need to monitor carefully the results of the marketing wars that take place every day of the week and year.

GE was a good place to learn, but no place to stay. Nobody ever got promoted out of the advertising department into anything else. In those days it would hire 50 college graduates a year just for the advertising department. They were replacing those who left, but what happened was that people stayed two, three, four or five years and then said, 'Hmm, I can only go so far here so I'm going to leave.' There was a very, very definite prejudice against non-engineers becoming a manager of anything decent at GE.

What did 'marketing' look like at the company?

That's a good point. There were two kinds of marketing jobs at GE: one was in the advertising department, the other – advertising and marketing – within the product divisions. Engineers primarily filled those jobs in the product divisions. They were at least on track to get promoted and become a divisional manager or something like that, but they didn't do very much advertising, nor very much marketing.

We were kind of like an internal advertising agency. So you didn't learn much advertising if you worked for a product division, but you learned a lot in the advertising and sales promotion department, which is what it was called. You wrote ads, you did brochures, slide films, movies and posters – a

lot of stuff. I learned a lot about the preparation of advertising and marketing materials working there, but it became obvious pretty quickly that if you
wanted to stay in the same job for 50 years, sure, you could stay there, but
I wasn't interested in that.

Did it give you a good grounding for founding your own agency?

Yes, that and the two advertising agencies I worked for in New York before
I founded my own.

**What have been the challenges you faced in getting these concepts
understood over the years?**

Positioning is an accepted concept, although many organizations practise it
in a way that we might not totally agree with. Focus is different. Very few
companies practise it. Very few companies agree with its principles. Broadening the line, broadening the appeal, broadening the distribution are all so
logical that who can disagree?

Focus is illogical and very difficult to sell. Paradoxically, that makes the
concept extremely valuable. If every company were focused, it would be difficult to develop an effective marketing strategy for any individual company.
The competition would be just too powerful. The fact that few companies
are truly focused creates enormous opportunities and enormous potential.

In truth, what value is there in a concept that is universally accepted?
'We love our customers' is a claim that many, many companies make. Who
can possibly disagree with that concept? And what value does that concept
have? Very little. Who can build a powerful company around that sort of
generality? And that's the trouble with most marketing concepts. They're
universally accepted. Everyone practises them. But no one company can use
them to build a powerful strategy.

Take the internet, for example. Early on, when it was almost totally
ignored by established companies, a number of entrepreneurs were able to
build powerful brands (and make billions of dollars) with websites such as
Yahoo!, Amazon.com, eBay, America Online, Google and others.

Do those same opportunities exist today? Of course not. Everybody
accepts the general principle that the internet is one of the most effective
communication tools in the world. It's true, but not of much use to any one
company.

Current views of marketing

To be successful, you've said it's important for companies to look for gaps in people's minds, and then focus on them. Is this too simplistic?

No, marketing is, in many cases, simple. It's not easy, but it's simple. But it's very hard to stand for something if you stand for everything. It's also interesting that people always mistake perception for reality.

For example, when we were at GE, we noticed that many big companies were unsuccessful when they tried to get into markets where they possessed no credibility: GE in mainframe computers; Western Union in telephone service; and Xerox in computers. Conventional wisdom said that these and other companies failed to expand their lines because their products were no match for the competition. Having worked for GE, however, I knew this wasn't true. It wasn't a product problem. It was a perception problem.

All of life is perception. There is no reality. The average person considers reality to be whatever impressions are formed in that person's mind. Which, of course, are only perceptions. Dealing with perception is the number one problem in life, whether you are marketing a product or marketing yourself.

This concept is exceptionally useful for a marketing person. It gives you great flexibility in dealing with problems. Does a product have a bad name? Then change it. Don't try to change perceptions, which are very difficult to do. Too many marketing people get bogged down with 'facts'. They know everything about their products, their competition, the distribution, etc. All of these 'facts' combine to greatly restrict their options.

> *All of life is perception. There is no reality. The average person considers reality to be whatever impressions are formed in that person's mind. Which, of course, are only perceptions. Dealing with perception is the number one problem in life, whether you are marketing a product or marketing yourself. This concept is exceptionally useful for a marketing person. It gives you great flexibility in dealing with problems. Does a product have a bad name? Then change it. Don't try to change perceptions, which are very difficult to do.*

Successful marketing people deal with perceptions only. These are the only things that matter, in marketing or in life.

Can you elaborate on that?

Here in the USA, for example, I've talked to a number of people who say, 'Well, the problem with General Motors (GM) is that it doesn't make good cars.' And believe me, they have very, very strong beliefs that GM makes lousy cars. So I ask them whether they've ever owned one.

'Well, I wouldn't buy one,' comes the reply.

'Why's that? Are you an automotive engineer?'

No, they're not.

'Have they ever driven one?'

No. 'Well, how do you know that?'

'Well, I know.'

People possess very strong opinions without really having done much personal investigation. They believe what they read in the paper. If a magazine or newspaper says that GM makes lousy cars, it makes lousy cars. So it's all perception, and one of the problems of business in general is that it's very hard to have a strong perception if you're a manufacturing generalist rather than a specialist. If, for some reason, a company just makes one product it's perceived to be a specialist and therefore better.

Take the medical community: I'm talking about the difference between a general practitioner and a specialist. Everybody just assumes a specialist is better. A cardiologist must know more about the heart. A doctor starting out as a specialist in cardiology, with no experience, will be perceived to know more about the heart than a GP who's been in business for 50 years, and probably knows a lot about it. But of course he or she's not a specialist.

Everybody just assumes that the specialist knows more than the generalist. These are some of the perceptions that cloud people's ability to know what is and what's not the best product. So focus is one aspect.

For the other, let's take Sony. Sony makes everything. It might have a terrific feature in television sets, in computers or let's say in video game players. That might add up to a lot of product benefits across its line, but are people going to remember that?

Volvo, meanwhile, makes safe cars. If it were to make washing machines, refrigerators, TV sets and everything else, people would find it very hard to hang an attribute like safety on the Volvo brand. It's even harder to hang any one attribute on the Sony brand except that it's been around forever, it's one of the biggest Japanese consumer electronics companies, and it's a powerful worldwide brand. But it's not known for anything.

In your view, what corporate qualities do you need to be able to make the grade?

We're big believers in strong centralized management. In other words, management of the strategy should be centralized, but the tactics, the details, can be decentralized. And we find that companies get in trouble when they decentralize strategic decisions.

GM, for example, is, I think, in trouble because it lets its brands decide what kind of cars to sell instead of saying, 'OK – now you're entry level, you're a step above and you're premium' and so on.

As a result, all GM brands try to be everything to everybody. Chevrolet sells cheap cars and expensive cars. Cadillac was an expensive brand but is now trying to sell cheap cars. And though Chevrolet used to be an entry level brand, GM has now also introduced the Saturn. So what is its entry level brand? They've got two of them.

These are strategic errors that strong, centralized management would never have allowed to happen. You can't, however, run a big company from the centre and try to manage all the details. You have to leave them up to individual managers. But there is a combination there: GM is too decentralized yet, on the other hand, companies like GE are too centralized and I think, long term, that's going to get it in trouble. But we'll see what happens.

You've said before that if every company were focused it would be difficult to develop an effective marketing strategy for any individual company. Would you expand on this?

Well, take automobiles: Volvo stands for safety; BMW for driving; Mercedes Benz for prestige. There are dozens of brands, but aside from those three it's very hard to tell what's a Buick, a Chevrolet or a Volkswagen these days. So in a massive industry like automobiles there are only a few brands that are focused. This leaves a lot of opportunities for other brands to jump in with different types of focus – yet they can't. It's the perception versus reality idea.

When you've established a powerful position – like Volvo has with safety – nobody can take it away. We have an insurance institute for highway safety that tests all these automobiles and they pick the 10 safest cars currently available. How many do you think were Volvos? None. Do you think that changes people's perception? Not at all. People still think Volvos are a safe car. It doesn't matter what the insurance institute for highway safety says. It's perception versus reality.

Look at it from the opposite point of view. What drives business today is expansion. Companies want to grow, but in the process they risk becoming unfocused, getting into more products and services.

So what's the solution?

It's to launch second, third and fourth brands. So why don't they? Because we have a number of myths in business today. One is that launching a new brand is expensive – which is why it's done so rarely.

Our stance is that you shouldn't spend a lot of money on advertising to launch a new brand, you should use PR. It's a lot less expensive. Advertising is not a good tactic to use when you have neither credibility, nor believability. Why would I read an ad about a brand I've never heard about? It can't be any good, right? Because I've never heard of it.

This is one of the real reasons that companies don't want second brands: because they say it's too expensive. Furthermore, they don't want to launch a new brand until the market is big enough. Another myth. Guess what? When the market is big enough it's too late. It means somebody else has got there first.

Why do so many companies still do line extensions?

The dangers of line extensions were dramatized in *Positioning* and in every other book that I have been involved with. Is this an accepted idea in the marketing community? Not at all. If anything, line extension is considered a good thing to do. Many companies spend thousands of dollars researching potential line-extension ideas for their brands.

We've argued with so many top management people on this very issue. Trying to sell Xerox mainframe computers? That didn't work. We argued with Western Union when they got in the telephone business. That didn't work.

The argument is always the same. Launch a new brand. 'Yeah, I know, but our research says that if we launch a new brand people won't buy it because they've never heard of the brand.' Well, that's true, but you've got to have a little faith that you can use marketing techniques to make people aware of the brand. A good example is Red Bull. At its launch, research showed that people hated the product, its name, everything about it. Now it's a market leader.

How do you stop companies making the same mistake?

When we work with an entrepreneur who wants to compete with some of the largest companies in the world, it helps to tell the Dell story. If Michael Dell can successfully compete with IBM – at the time it was the most powerful company worldwide – then almost anyone can. Provided, of course, that the entrepreneur is willing to narrow the focus.

Dell narrowed its focus to selling PCs direct by phone: simple, powerful, and effective. Yet it's a very difficult idea to sell to a big, established company. 'What? You want to limit the market for our new product to direct sales only? When nobody else is doing this? And, therefore, there's no established market for selling this product direct?'

Most companies today are focused on doing things better when success is always found by doing things differently.

If you had to put forward one case study to illustrate how a company/organization can get it right, and another how one can get it wrong, which ones would they be and why?

Nokia got it right and Eastman Kodak got it wrong.

Nokia once made everything all under the Nokia name: paper, chemicals, rubber products (including tyres and boots), electronics, machinery, computers and cell phones. Then, when the cell phone business started to take off, Nokia made an incredibly brave and smart decision. It decided to focus on cell phones and get out of everything else. This helped it become the world's largest cell phone manufacturer, with around a 35% share internationally.

Eastman Kodak got it wrong. Kodak was the world leader in film photography, but the market has been changing to digital. So what did Kodak do? It decided to transform the Kodak brand into a digital one. Kodak's chairman, George Fisher, said at the time: 'This announcement marks the first step in our strategy to move the Kodak brand name into the electronic world.'

But you can't move a brand name, especially one like Kodak, which is so deeply imbedded in prospects' minds. What should it have done? Launch a second brand to cover the digital market. This is the strategy used successfully by Toyota when it launched the Lexus brand to cover the high end automobile market. Lexus has become the largest-selling luxury car brand in America.

Companies are missing a trick. They know brands are important. They're just not making the connection between a brand standing for something. Everybody thinks their brand is Virgin. I always say, 'You're not Richard Branson and your brand ain't Virgin. If you're willing to get out there and do all the silly PR stunts that Richard is doing then fine, maybe you can make your brand as successful as Virgin.'

How can people identify fads as opposed to important new techniques?

Easy. Fads take off rapidly, trends slowly. A few years ago magazines and newspapers were full of stories about the merits of a low-carb diet. Thousands of low-carb products were introduced in the marketplace. Today, almost all these products have been withdrawn from the market.

On the other hand, trends take off very slowly. Look at the Red Bull energy drink. It took five years for it to break $10m in sales and another four to break $100m. Today it does $2bn in worldwide sales.

Many, many other major brands have also taken off very slowly: Southwest Airlines, Wal-Mart stores, to name just a few. What should a company do if one of its products or brands starts to take off rapidly? Dampen sales by restricting distribution, cutting back production, raising prices, etc. Don't let the brand turn into a fad.

Your latest ideas revolve around the idea of divergence. How does it apply to the way companies should be operating?

First, let me tell you what I mean. Our latest book, *The Origin of Brands*, is dedicated to 'Divergence, the least understood and most important force in the universe'. Laura and I are spending much of our time promoting this 'divergence' concept, which we borrowed from Charles Darwin.

Our basic premise is that, over time, categories diverge and become two or more categories, creating endless opportunities to build new brands. It's these endless opportunities that make marketing such an exciting business. Oddly enough, one of the things I remember vividly was when television was first introduced. People talked about convergence: newspapers would become obsolete, they'd be printed out of your TV set but only those sections that you wanted to read.

This was the big benefit: if you wanted to read the sports section you went and printed it out. This got an amazing amount of publicity at the time. Yet if you told people that story today, most of them would look at you and say: 'That's ridiculous.' It is, however, a typical convergence idea.

That one example opened my mind to the possibility that, despite all the hype about convergence devices in general, they're unlikely to be commercially successful. We've been fighting this issue for years, because, from a research and development point of view, it really penalizes a company. Papers are full of stories about the big consumer electronics companies spending 90 % of their research dollars trying to converge. Yet a look in the history books shows that almost exactly the opposite has been happening. Go through almost any category and see how, over time, invariably things diverge.

So you're not just talking about technology?

No, it's not just about technology. For example, Anheuser-Busch introduced B to the E, a brand of beer with caffeine and that Brazilian energy stuff, guarana. And Philips introduced an electric toothbrush with toothpaste in the device itself. And Oakley introduced a line of sunglasses with MP3 players. I'll guarantee that all of these things will fail, but they capture the public's imagination, that's the problem.

It's the flying car phenomenon. Write about a flying car and everybody says, 'Wow, I really like that concept.' They don't think about the problems, just that it sounds great. Likewise, so many of these convergence devices sound terrific and, because of the publicity, some are selling. Take smart phones. Millions of these have sold, but the truth is iPod sales, *the* divergence device, far outstrip them. The other thing is people don't see the divergence, or where these new technologies come from.

Let's change tack slightly. What's your view of the state of marketing these days?

Marketing is in trouble today. The marketing function gets little credit for the success or failure of companies. Instead the focus is on management, not marketing. Yet I think marketing is the most important function in a corporation.

Take Jack Welch. He was recently named 'manager of the century' by *Fortune* magazine. Yet what does he say about marketing in his latest book *Winning*, co-authored by his wife Suzy? Absolutely nothing. He does give, however, human resources (HR) much of the credit for a company's success. 'The head of HR,' he says, 'should be the second most important person in any organization.'

There are several other indications that the marketing function is in trouble. *Fortune* magazine, for example, picked the 75 best business books of the past 75 years. How many of these books were marketing books? Absolutely none. Apparently *Fortune* doesn't think that marketing is important.

Then there's the relatively new position of chief marketing officer (CMO) that some companies have adopted. According to a study released in October 2005 by Spencer Stuart, an executive search firm, the average tenure of a chief marketing officer is 22.9 months. This is hardly an endorsement for the marketing function.

But isn't one of the problems that many chief executive officers (CEOs) don't understand the importance of marketing?

Our ideas, books and so forth have been accepted among advertising and marketing people within companies – but not their top management. So the challenge isn't so much to sell the ideas to the marketing community, but to top management.

I had dinner recently with Phil Kotler and we talked about the same thing. If a CEO has a legal problem he turns to his lawyers and says, 'What do you think?' If he has a financial problem he turns to the chief financial officer (CFO) and says, 'What do you think?' But if he has a marketing problem he turns to the marketing people and says, 'This is what I want to do,' because he sees marketing as simply common sense.

> *Marketing is in trouble today. The marketing function gets little credit for the success or failure of companies. Instead the focus is on management, not marketing. Yet I think marketing is the most important function in a corporation.*

To what extent is this the fault of marketers?

Marketing people have been quick to exploit the new technologies such as the internet to promote and sell products. Every year the tactics of marketing get better and better, but the strategies have not kept pace. Too often marketing people have to accept the strategies dictated by their management.

If I were a marketing professor, I would give marketing tactics an 'A' and marketing strategy a 'C minus'.

What makes a good marketer?

A great marketing person is a rare combination of a specialist and a generalist. To become a great marketing person, you need to know everything about business in general *and* gain a detailed knowledge of a specific industry.

Apart from marketers having to gain more credibility in the organization, what do you think are the biggest challenges facing marketing generally?

The biggest challenge is the global challenge. The world is becoming one big market. If a company doesn't 'go global', foreign competitors will enter its market and take away its business. In the long run, there will only be global brands and local brands. In-between brands face an uncertain future.

The other problem is the rising power of distribution. Companies like Wal-Mart can make or break a brand. Distribution today is a big, big problem in marketing and will continue to be so for small and medium-size companies. Many of them can manufacture good products at reasonable prices, but can't get the distribution to make their brands successful and the problem is getting worse.

When you think about brands and prices, you can't ignore distribution. In fact, one of the things that works very well is a focus on distribution. In other words, don't try to get your brand in every outlet. Go to one of the drug stores or a supermarket and, if you have a new brand, say: 'Look, I'll give you this new brand exclusively for six months or a year, but I want displays or something.'

Work with a distribution outlet exclusively, as some people have done with Wal-Mart very successfully. In a sense, they're getting Wal-Mart to endorse the product and handle it exclusively for a year or so, which gets the brand off the ground. That's one of the ways around this 'we need $50m to launch it with advertising'. That's why a focus on distribution is one of our core ideas when launching a new brand.

Getting more personal

What were the main influences on your work?

The 'what' is easy. It was 30 years of experience that taught me what works and what doesn't work in advertising.

What was there in your background that made you so willing to focus so deeply on something and stick to it?

Well, I guess I don't necessarily agree with somebody just because they happen to have a bigger job, a bigger reputation or make more money than I do. I only agree with people when I think it's right to do so. I'm very willing to argue, and I've done so with the CEOs of a lot of companies – including Digital Equipment and Xerox – about what should or should not be done. I don't just assume that because they're chief executive they know more than I do.

Well, I guess I don't necessarily agree with somebody just because they happen to have a bigger job, a bigger reputation or make more money than I do. I only agree with people when I think it's right to do so. I'm very willing to argue, and I've done so with the CEOs of a lot of companies . . . about what should or should not be done. I don't just assume that because they're chief executive they know more than I do.

Do you ever feel bemused that your name is so well known around the world?

I didn't think this would happen. I thought that we could run a successful business, but I never thought I'd become someone that people would know about worldwide. That's just kind of a spin-off from our books and articles, plus the strength of our ideas, too. That's a good thing and we continue to work on that. One of the exciting things about business, and about marketing too, is there are always new things to learn.

What is it like working with your daughter now?

Absolutely terrific. I know that everything I do will still be useful even if I'm not around. As a matter of fact, we're building a brand here and it's a classic example of how to do it. We're making the Ries brand stand for marketing in people's minds and I think that my daughter, Laura – who is very, very talented – will be a lot more famous than I ever was.

Really?

I think that she's got the ability and a head start, too. I kind of started from nothing. She's very well grounded and has basically found her roots. Many marketing people are too blue sky. One of the discussions I had with Phil Kotler was about a marketing person he'd met here in Atlanta who runs one of the creative boutiques.

He was telling me about this guy's idea to create something above the brand, an overall concept that transcends the brand itself. My own feeling is that what works in marketing is bringing things down to earth. That will make you billions of dollars without having these blue sky ideas that nobody can quite understand.

Do you think that reading *The Hucksters* about advertising was the defining moment in your life?

The Hucksters just pointed me in the direction of advertising. I think that, as a result of reading that book, I became more aware of the advertising around me. But it turned out to be more than just advertising. Human communication is the most interesting, most difficult and most challenging activity you can possibly undertake.

How do you convince another person to buy a product? To buy an idea? To buy a concept? This is a continuing challenge for everybody whether you are a business leader, a politician, a spouse or a parent.

What are you proudest of in terms of your work?

I think it has to be our latest book, *The Origin of Brands*. It's the most original, most useful book we have ever written. Unfortunately, it has not received the publicity that many of our other books have received. But no matter.

I've always felt that if each book didn't take things a step further then we shouldn't be writing it in the first place. So I think the latest book is by far the most important one. I also think that the future belongs not only to divergence, but to brands.

Selected publications

The Origin of Brands, HarperCollins, 2004. Co-author: Laura Ries.

The 22 Immutable Laws of Branding, HarperCollins, 2003, 1998. Co-author: Laura Ries.

The Fall of Advertising and the Rise of PR, HarperCollins, 2002. Co-author: Laura Ries.

Positioning, 20th anniversary edn, McGraw-Hill, 2000. Co-author: Jack Trout.

The 11 Immutable Laws of Internet Branding, HarperCollins, 2000. Co-author: Laura Ries.

Focus: The Future of Your Company Depends on It, HarperCollins, 1996.

The 22 Immutable Laws of Marketing, HarperCollins, 1993. Co-author: Jack Trout.

Horse Sense: The Key to Success is Finding a Horse to Ride, McGraw-Hill, 1991. Co-author: Jack Trout.

Bottom-Up Marketing, McGraw-Hill, 1989. Co-author: Jack Trout.

Marketing Warfare, McGraw-Hill, 1986. Co-author: Jack Trout.

Positioning: The Battle for Your Mind, McGraw-Hill, 1981. Co-author: Jack Trout.

8

....

Don Schultz

Integrated marketing
communications innovator

Don E. Schultz is Professor Emeritus-in-Service of Integrated Marketing Communications at the Medill School, Northwestern University. He is also President of the consulting firm, Agora, Inc. both in Evanston, Illinois. Additionally, he is a visiting professor at Cranfield School of Management, Bedfordshire, UK; Adjunct Professor at Queensland University of Technology, Brisbane, Australia; and Visiting Professor, Tsinghua University, Beijing, China.

Following his graduation from the University of Oklahoma with a degree in marketing/journalism, he began his career as a sales promotion writer for trade magazine publishers in Dallas. From there, he moved into publication sales and management and was advertising director of a daily newspaper in Texas. He then joined Tracy-Locke Advertising and Public Relations in Dallas in 1965. He was with the agency for almost 10 years as branch manager in its Dallas, New York and Columbus, Ohio, offices. He was a management supervisor for a number of national consumer products, service and industrial accounts.

In 1974, he resigned as senior vice president of the agency to move into academia. He received an MA in advertising and a PhD in mass media from Michigan State University while teaching in the department of advertising. He joined Northwestern in 1977.

Schultz has consulted, lectured and held seminars on integrated marketing communication (IMC), marketing, advertising, sales promotion, brands and branding, and communication management in Europe, South America, Asia, the Middle East, Australia and North America. His articles have appeared in numerous professional trade publications and academic journals. He was the founding editor of the Journal of Direct Marketing *and serves as the associate editor of the* Journal of Marketing Communications. *He is also on the editorial review board for a number of trade and scholarly publications. He was named one of the 80 Most Influential People in sales and marketing in the world by* Sales and Marketing Management *magazine in 1998.*

He is author/co-author of eighteen books, including Strategic Advertising Campaigns *(now in its 5th edition),* Essentials of Advertising Strategy *(now in its 3rd edition), and* Measuring Brand Communication ROI. *Other books include* Communicating Globally, 2000, *and* Raising the Corporate Umbrella, 2001. *He and his wife Heidi have published an update on the seminal text on IMC,* Integrated Marketing Communication: Next Generation, *which was published in 2003. They also have co-authored* Brand Babble: Sense and Nonsense about Brands and Branding *which was also published in 2004.*

He serves on the board of directors of Brand Finance plc, in London, UK, and is on the advisory board of a number of marketing and communication organiz- ations. He also provides consultancy services to a broad variety of marketing organizations, agencies, media and nonprofit organizations around the world.

The professional journey

Let's take a look at your history. Why the shift to academia?

I had spent 15 years in business after graduating from the University of Oklahoma, the last 10 with an advertising agency. Then a few things hap- pened. First, I realized that the advertising business, much as those in it would like to think it's exciting, is essentially repetitive, at least on the man- agement side. You do the same thing year after year after year. You make the commercials, you show the commercials, and then you start all over again. After you've done that for a while, you begin to think – 'Well, there's got to be more to it than this.'

Another thing was, because I was in a vertical progression system, I even- tually ended up as a senior vice president. That actually meant I was running a group of branch offices and not doing much of anything connected to actual advertising. I would be looking at what kind of telephone system we had, what kind of copier we needed and, the worst one of all, who got to sit by the window.

Finally, I had been telling clients all this time that you had to spend more money and buy more ads. And they kept asking, 'Why?' And I would say, 'Because you just have to.' I really didn't know why and I think that's still pretty true of most agency people. We did advertising so more was always better. So, I thought: 'Well, I'll go back to school and see if I can figure out why.' I went back to school and I did my graduate work at Michigan State University. I was awarded a master's degree in advertising in 1975 and six months later I knew I wanted to finish my PhD and remain in teaching. In 1977, after I got my doctorate, I was offered a teaching job in Northwest- ern University's graduate advertising program.

What were you interested in particularly?

I was at Michigan State at a very unique time. It had an interdisciplinary PhD program in the College of Communication Arts and Sciences. That included telecommunication, journalism, advertising and mass communication, which no one else in the country or even the world was doing. That was the mid-1970s. The big thing was our focus on information technology. We were starting to get data from supermarket scanner panels so, for the first time, we could actually look at what people were doing and how they were responding to specific communication programs. That changed my life forever.

I got very interested in advertising response and advertising response models: how you can determine and justify what advertising you should be doing by examining whether or not it worked and why. A lot of that early work involved the impact and effect of sales promotion, so I got deeply involved in that and in data analytics. My PhD was about mass media impact, focusing on advertising response functions.

Traditional advertising said you have to see things two or three times before they are effective. But I found that the first exposure was often the most valuable. With the next you get less return, and then it flattens out pretty quickly. This wasn't well received by the advertising business because agencies were making money by getting clients to spend more money on media, the premise being that you needed frequency to be effective.

At the same time there was the big explosion in cable television in the USA, so we had the beginnings of interactive communications for the first time. It was all very experimental and very exciting. For example, we had a grant to run a demonstration project to train firemen in Rockford, IL. Those of us in East Lansing, which is where the university was, could talk about and show techniques to the firemen in Rockford, about 500 miles away and in another state. They could then send back answers in real time. From that experience, I became very interested in information technology.

Actually, if you look at what I've done, the pattern is fairly obvious. I started with advertising response functions. Then, I began to look at scanner data and sales promotion. It's not a big

In the mid-1980s I started to think, 'Well, gee, all of this stuff is converging. How can people tell whether they saw an ad, or whether they responded to a promotion, or whether it was a PR story or something else?' That's when I began to think more about integrated marketing communication.

leap from sales promotion to data analytics and on to database marketing. From there I got very involved in direct marketing. I was the founding editor of the *Journal of Direct Marketing*. Then, in the mid-1980s I started to think, 'Well, gee, all of this stuff is converging. How can people tell whether they saw an ad, or whether they responded to a promotion, or whether it was a PR story or something else?' That's when I began to think more about integrated marketing communication.

What was the wider context at the time?

In the late 1980s it was fairly obvious big changes were occurring. All of the ad agencies were consolidating, with big agencies buying smaller ones. Clients were beginning to move their money from advertising to direct marketing, PR and sales promotion. The answer for advertising agencies was to acquire and consolidate. They started to say, 'What we'll do is create one-stop shopping by buying a PR agency, a direct marketing agency, and so on. We'll put them all under one roof and we can then offer clients whatever they want.'

In the mid-1980s, I was chairman of the graduate advertising department at Northwestern. In that group, we also had corporate public relations and direct marketing sequences. We thought, 'Let's bring all this together.' So, my associates and I went to the university president and said: 'This is what we want to do because we think this is the direction for the future.' Fortunately, we had a very far-sighted president who replied, 'If you think it will work, I'll fund it.' He gave us $100,000 to get it going. I actually wrote the first IMC curriculum on my dining room table.

Had you looked around to see if there was anything like that anywhere else?

Having been very closely involved in advertising and marketing communication education, I knew there wasn't anything like this being done anywhere.

Nowhere?

Nowhere. No one even talked about integration. Everywhere you went, people would say these are all separate disciplines, separate concepts, separate ideas. So that's where we started. Our first degrees from Northwestern's Medill IMC program were awarded in 1991 and we have been doing it ever since.

How did you come to write your book on integrated marketing communications?

In 1989 I had received a telephone call from two people: John O'Toole, who was executive vice president of the American Association of Advertising Agencies (AAAA) and Keith Reinhart, who was the AAAA chairman for the year. They said, 'We are trying to figure out what to do with this integrated marketing communication world. The ad agencies have all gone out and bought agencies in other disciplines, but they can't get them to work together.' They asked if I would come and help them work on that. In 1989, integration meant four things: advertising, sales promotion, direct marketing and PR. So they gave us a grant to do a research study that included AAAA, the Association of National Advertisers and the American Advertising Federation.

To provide a basis for what we had learned, three of us decided to write a book, *Integrated Marketing Communications: Putting It Together and Making It Work*, which was published in 1993. I was the lead author. The co-authors were Stan Tannenbaum, who was also teaching at Medill – he had been chairman of an ad agency before moving to a client company as an executive vice president – and Robert Lauterborn, who had worked for International Paper Company and GE before he became a chaired professor of advertising at the University of North Carolina.

Are more universities now adopting this approach?

It depends on how you define IMC. Yes, there are a lot who are teaching their version of IMC courses and some of them have a degree program. For instance, we have a cooperative agreement for the first time with Queensland University of Technology in Australia, and we are starting to exchange students and faculty. And that works very well because there is a common culture, and we're talking about much the same thing. Australia is about at the same level as the USA. The only difference is that it's a long, long way off. We're also looking at setting up similar programs in India and we have had some conversations with the Chinese.

What about in Europe?

A very limited number. In the UK, Luton and Hull Universities have programs as well as some others.

Why do you think that is?

Well, I believe it is because integration is anathema to the Western management style. There is a book by Richard Nisbett called *Geography of Thought: How Asians and Westerners Think Differently – and Why*. It argues that all Western culture comes from the ancient Greeks, who lived on islands which were continually beset by different peoples passing through. So the Greeks essentially created a thought process which was based on categorization and differentiation. He argues that Eastern thinking, on the other hand, came from China's Middle Kingdom, which had very little outside influence and was more holistic. So the Greeks are atomistic, while the Eastern cultures are holistic.

So, when I go to China and Japan and talk about integration, they look at me and ask, 'Why would you not do that?' When I go to Europe, they say, 'Why would you do that?'

What about in the USA?

It's exactly the same thing. The USA is dominated by Western thought patterns. That's the reason I tell the Chinese, 'If you want to succeed in the global marketplace please don't copy Western management approaches because they are all trying to reinvent themselves. You don't need to do that.'

And they reply, 'OK, but look at how successful companies like Procter & Gamble are.'

I tell them that all those companies are urgently trying to change, so you, the Chinese, have an opportunity to do it right the first time, rather than doing it the wrong way and then trying to change it the way Western companies are doing.

When your first book came out, were you a voice in the wilderness, so to speak?

To a certain extent. There was a huge amount of interest in IMC. But, when I explained the approach, they would say, 'This is really hard to do. Let's just stay with what we're doing now.'

Is it getting any better?

Well, it's true that practically no organization will argue that communications should be disintegrated. They agree that they have to do something. But the problem is they don't know how. A lot of this change has been driven by technology. That's particularly true in marketing communication. Look at the huge explosion of media systems. You used to have someone whose only decision was whether to put money into advertising or sales promotion, and maybe do a bit of PR, and if they could get a list they'd mail people something.

That's all changed. We are currently working on a research project called 'simultaneous media usage'. Think about this. When you are online, you can also be watching TV, reading the newspaper and talking on the cell phone – all at the same time. In these studies, we have 28 different forms of media. We can't talk about individual media activities any more. That means we have to start thinking about how the consumer deals with all that, and what impact and effect it has.

It also affects measurement systems. When you are multi-tasking with media, are you counted as a quarter of a person because you are doing four media things at once? Or do we count you as 100% for each of the four, which is what we do now, and get to 400% usage? The systems just ignore any kind of simultaneous exposure because we measure each medium separately.

In addition, we don't have a clue about the synergy between each of them. For instance, do they work together or do they work independently? Do they help or hurt each other? Some of the work we have been doing shows that in some cases $1 + 1 + 1$ doesn't equal three but around nine. And, in other cases, some combinations of three media equal a -1. It all depends.

Current views of marketing

Why do you think so many companies seem to be struggling in today's environment?

Let me go back a bit. In the mid-1990s I began to think about brands and branding. I realized that people don't really have relationships with companies, they have relationships with brands. And the brand, of course, is simply an agglomeration of everything the company has done and what experience the consumer has had with the brand. In 2001 I had what I guess I'd call my biggest epiphany. I realized that whenever we talk about marketing we mean outbound messaging and promotion. It assumes that we, as marketers, control the marketplace and when we send stuff out in its latest form we can control and manage it.

We tried to call that customer relationship 'management'. But truthfully, today, we are not managing customers. They are managing us. So that got me into my current activities, which are about trying to determine how you connect internal and external marketing. In 2003 we started to focus on internal marketing and got some outside funding to do research.

Was this the first time you had become involved in internal marketing?

Yes, everything we had done up to that point had been about external. I wanted to put a course together and thought, 'Well, I'll get all the literature for the students to read.' And that took all of 20 minutes because there was so little. No one ever talks about their employees – certainly not in marketing. That's the job of human resources (HR).

The problem is that there are few programs about how to get employees aligned with their organization's goals and objectives. That's what I'm working on now. The interesting thing I've found is that in some organizations internal marketing comes under marketing. In some it's under corporate communications. And, in still others, it's under HR. So you have all these employees wandering around inside the firm asking: 'What is this company doing? Why are we here? Why won't anybody tell me what our strategy is?'

The management then looks at them and says, 'Well, you work here so you ought to know that.'

Not a very helpful solution.

But you have to get employees carefully aligned with the strategy. They have to know it and understand it. A lot of this has come out of services businesses where the employees really are critical. As long as most companies were basically manufacturing-based, it didn't really matter what employees did. In fact, we could treat them as badly as we wanted to as long as they turned out good products and we had good distribution. That's why the 4Ps – product, place, price and promotion – worked.

I have been trying to get rid of those 4Ps for a long time. But they simply won't die. We are still teaching the 4Ps in every business school around the world. You can't get a marketing book published unless it is based on the 4Ps approach. And the reason is relatively simple. It's very easy to teach the 4Ps.

Now, I've had a number of conversations with Phil Kotler about this. In fact, he is one of my biggest supporters. But he says, 'Well, I can't put what you are talking about into my textbooks until it is common practice. So you go out there and make it work and then I'll include it in my textbooks.' However, if you look at Phil's books over the years, he actually began to pick up on integration in about 1994 and has been expanding his views with almost every edition.

The point is, when you start to bring the internal marketing focus in, what you quickly realize is that marketing is not something that a department does. It's what the organization does. Very few marketing people think about marketing as a corporate activity. What they are really focused on is: 'How do I create a marketing function within the organization and get more power and prestige?' And this is where I come to a divergence with traditional marketing people. When I argue that marketing is what the organization does, it forces you out of the vertical, functional silos and forces you to think and work horizontally. That is very, very difficult in traditional organizational structures.

What I struggle with today is that 'integration' is likely the wrong term. It was probably right for the late 1980s and early 1990s, but not today. Quite honestly, sometimes I wish I'd never written that first book with Stan and Bob. The reason is we looked at integration as getting things to look the same, feel the same and be the same in all outbound communication. But that's not what integration is in a multimedia, multi-promotion, global marketplace. Integration is about alignment. Because the real issue today is how to align the organization. You're not going to break down the silos. The best you can hope to do is to align them so they work together.

One of the problems is that organizations say, 'Well, we've got everybody to agree on a corporate colour, we all agree on a standard business card, a corporate logo, a corporate sound bite, so we've done integration. Now let's move on to something else.' What they don't understand is that integration is not something you do and move on. It has to be continuous; it takes a long time and it forces the whole organization to change. And, basically, functional specialists don't like change.

Most managers and certainly most marketing specialists don't want to hear that. If you've been a functional manager for 15 years, and I come in and say, 'You're going to have to change your way of working' it sounds like I'm the anti-Christ. But, then again, there's a certain reward for that because you do get visibility by being the anti-Christ. Not love, but perhaps some questioning recognition among senior managers.

What I struggle with today is that 'integration' is likely the wrong term. It was probably right for the late 1980s and early 1990s, but not today . . . The reason is we looked at integration as getting things to look the same, feel the same and be the same in all outbound communication. But that's not what integration is in a multimedia, multi-promotion, global marketplace. Integration is about alignment. Because the real issue today is how to align the organization.

So you no longer want to use the word 'integration'?

'Integration' is the wrong term, but I can't get rid of it. I'm the IMC guy, just like Al Ries and Jack Trout are the positioning guys and Lester Wunderman is the direct marketing guy. Anyway, what I'm really doing now is trying to look at how you can integrate. But it's not a communication integration process as much as how you align the whole organization. We know that if you have customers, it's not the marketing people who have all the impact on them. It's also the financial people, the HR people, the operations people – it's across the board. It's an organizational thing.

The problem, I find, is that too many marketing people want to be a functional group inside the organization. But that marginalizes marketing's role. Because if you say that marketing is over there, and is responsible for customers and communications, it allows the rest of the organization to say: 'OK, we don't have to worry about customers at all. That's marketing's job. So we don't have to worry about how product quality or customer service or delivery times impact customers. That's marketing's responsibility.'

As a result, senior management looks at marketing if something goes wrong and says, 'Well, that's your problem. You didn't do what you were supposed to do.'

So I believe that marketing, as it generally exists today, has created its own death spiral.

This probably hasn't been helped by senior management often not understanding what marketing is?

That's part of it. I can walk into any organization and ask senior management who the firm's top 10 customers are and they won't have a clue. They're focused on managing tangible assets, not customers. When I'm meeting with a board or senior management, or even with the marketing people, I ask one basic question: 'Who are your best customers? Name your ten best customers.' And they can't do it.

They'll name one or two, maybe they'll get to three, but very, very seldom will they be able to name the top 10. The reason for this is that they never think about customers. When they think about managing the organization they look at managing the tangible assets, not managing the intangible assets.

I suppose because it's easier?

Well, it's easier and that's what they've been trained to do. Remember that all our financial systems are essentially focused on managing tangible assets because the intangible ones don't show up on the balance sheets.

The other problem is that, by and large, marketing people have practically no training in finance and don't really understand how businesses operate. And some of the reason for that is that eons ago marketing people walked away from any kind of financial responsibility and focused on customer behaviour. This was back in the 1950s and 1960s.

When they did that, they then had to show that a focus on customer behaviour worked. So they searched around and adapted and adopted some behaviourist psychological models. 'OK,' they said, 'with these models we can do some survey research about how people feel, the opinions they have and the like and then we can sample and project onto the entire population. Maybe all we really have to do is talk regularly to half a dozen people in a focus group and then project that onto a nation of X million people.'

So we are victims of our own planning and processes. We've created the problem for ourselves.

Is finance included in the IMC curriculum?

We have finance/accounting courses in the curriculum now. In fact, we start the subject in the first term of study. And our students are asking for more. But we don't teach much traditional finance since that is based primarily on manufacturing. Essentially, we're teaching a specialized course on how to manage and evaluate intangible assets.

Are you increasingly knocking on an open door as understanding of all this spreads?

Well, the door is opening into different areas. Most of the time I spend now is with boards and financial people, because they are asking, 'What exactly are these marketing people doing? They are spending a ton of money and what's the result?'

I remember doing a seminar in Milan, where there were about 25 to 30 people in the room but not one marketing person. They were all chief executives (CEOs) and chief financial officers (CFOs) of major Italian organizations. And the whole discussion was about what their marketing people are doing, why they are doing it and how can we evaluate it. In short, the issues were what these senior people should know about marketing and how they could evaluate it.

Are there any sort of tips you might offer to those struggling to try and get some sort of marketing excellence into what they do?

I think the one thing that they have to understand is that the success of the company comes from only two sources: its customers and its employees. Not all the other stuff that's going on. It's not all the trappings, it's not the research and development, it's not the distribution systems, and it's not all the other things that go along with it. I don't think organizations pay enough attention to the fact that those are the only two places where income is generated. And companies either increase it or they dissipate it.

Finally, before we move to a more personal discussion, you mentioned China, which you visit quite regularly. Do you agree with accepted wisdom that it is going to be a huge force in the world economy?

It already is.

As you said before, culturally integration comes naturally?

Also, it's a planned economy so the Chinese can decide to do something and do it. The difficulty for them is the flip side of that: they have to start thinking about what customers want. They are very intrigued with the idea of brands and branding. If they can make a television set for $27, and then sell it in Shanghai for $35, or send it to the USA under a brand name and sell it for $135, they become very interested in marketing and branding. They have figured that out very quickly – they are a very bright people.

Most of the work we do is teaching in executive masters programs and primarily with Chinese companies, not multinationals. It's fun because the Chinese are saying to themselves, 'We've got to get into branding because we already know we can beat the rest of the world in terms of product costs.' In China, the goal is always to drive the price down. But 'Made in China' suffers somewhat from the same sort of stigma, and refers to the same quality problem that Japan had in the 1950s. So they want to take Chinese manufactured products and make them more acceptable.

We tell them they have several choices. They can build brands in the traditional way, as Haier is trying to do in the US with appliances and electronics. They can do what Lenovo has done, which is to buy a brand from elsewhere – in this case, IBM's PC business. Or they can buy retail distribution chains.

So what if they bought Wal-Mart? Not possible, you might think. But why not? They have more US dollars than anyone else in the world. They are making many of the products Wal-Mart carries. A group of Chinese companies could buy Wal-Mart and put all their products in under the Wal-Mart name and not need to build brands. The only question is whether the US

Government would raise the same sort of issues and restrictions as they did when the Chinese wanted to buy a US oil company. Would the US Government consider Wal-Mart a national resource and treasure?

Getting more personal

What is it about you, do you think, that made you so keen to teach?

Well, I think there's a teaching gene. My grandmother was a teacher, my mother was a teacher, my father was a football coach and a teacher for a while, so I think it's somewhere in the genes. My middle son was in broadcast television, he was an on-air newscaster for 12 years, and then decided he didn't like that any more and wanted to go back to school. So he went back to school, got a PhD and he's now teaching broadcast journalism at university.

My youngest son was a database and direct marketer with *Reader's Digest* and several other companies. About 10 years ago, he walked in and said, 'I think I'd like to be a minister' so he's gone into the ministry. So I think there must be a gene, there's got to be something in the family DNA that takes us in that direction.

I guess what I see as the big value of the academic area is that your services never go out of style or disappear. I still get letters, emails and notes from students from 15, 20 years ago which say, 'I just want to tell you that you had a huge impact on my life.' That's what makes it worthwhile. At one of my lectures a fellow walked up to me who was from Thailand. He was the student of one of my past students who had graduated about 20 years ago, who had encouraged him to come to Northwestern. That sort of thing gives you pleasure.

How much time do you spend teaching, as opposed to consultancy? Do you have a nice balance?

I think I do. Also, my wife was a magazine publisher, and about 10 years ago she got tired of me going off to exotic places so she left the publishing business and joined me in our consultancy, Agora Inc. Now we travel together doing seminars and teaching all over the world. We spend about 60% of our time out of the country.

That's a lot.

Well, I now have an appointment at Northwestern as an emeritus professor. My full title is Professor, Emeritus-in-Service, which means they retired me but they didn't want me to go away. So, in the fall, between September and December, I teach in the IMC program and she also teaches a branding course. And then the rest of the year we wander around. For instance, we spend two months in Australia because, if you've ever been to Chicago in the winter time, you'll know why we go to Australia. We are also spending a lot of time in China.

Is there something you might consider a defining moment in your life? One that got you on the path you're now on?

Well, many years ago, when I was an undergrad in university, there was a professor who had been in the agency business for a number of years. He had decided to go back and get his PhD. He started teaching, and he set up a joint interdisciplinary program where I was doing my undergraduate work. It was a major in marketing and a minor in journalism, actually advertising. He was a very, very innovative man and quite a leader. I just got interested in all the things that he was doing. Even after I graduated he kept in touch with me. He kept trying to get me to go back to school and do a graduate degree and that, to a certain extent, is what influenced me.

What are you proudest of in terms of your work?

Never having got fired! No, really, I think as much as anything, it's the ability to have some influence on the direction of the field and to try and develop some new concepts and approaches.

Which you haven't stopped doing yet?

Well, no, I haven't. And I hope I don't. That's probably, I think, the greatest satisfaction.

My work is more interesting now than it was 25 years ago, because 25 years ago all we were doing was tweaking established practices. Now, we're essentially reinventing the whole thing. That, to me, is the most intriguing aspect of it.

And you still find it as interesting as you did when you started?

More interesting now than it was 25 years ago, because 25 years ago all we were doing was tweaking established practices. Now, we're essentially reinventing the whole thing. That, to me, is the most intriguing aspect of it. If you look at the kinds of things I do, I guess it shows an entrepreneurial kind of spirit. But even though it looks like I'm all over the place, most of the things I do and am interested in are somehow interconnected. Maybe that's my approach to integration.

Selected publications

How to Sell More Stuff, Dearborn, 2005. Co-author: Steven Smith.

A Reader in Marketing Communications, Routledge, 2005. Co-authors: Philip Kitchen, Patrick de Pelsmacher and Lynne Eagle.

Brand Babble: Sense and Nonsense about Brands and Branding, South-Western, 2004. Co-author: Heidi F. Schultz.

Integrated Marketing Communication: The Next Generation, McGraw-Hill, 2003. Co-author: Heidi F. Schultz.

Raising the Corporate Umbrella, Palgrave, 2001. Co-author: Philip Kitchen.

Communicating Globally, NTC Business Books, 2000. Co-author: Philip Kitchen.

Measuring Brand Communication ROI, Association of National Advertisers, 1997. Co-author: Jeffrey Walters.

Integrated Marketing Communications: The New Marketing Paradigm, NTC Business Books, 1994. Co-authors: Stanley I. Tannenbaum and Robert Lauterborn.

Integrated Marketing Communications: Putting It Together And Making It Work, NTC Business Books, 1993. Co-authors: Stanley I. Tannenbaum and Robert Lauterborn

Strategic Newspaper Marketing, International Newspaper Marketing Association, 1990, 1993.

Sales Promotion Essentials, Crain Books, 1987. Co-author: William A. Robinson. (This text is now in its 3rd edn with various co-authors.)

Sales Promotion Management, Crain Books, 1982. Co-author: William A. Robinson.

Essentials of Advertising Strategy, Crain Books, 1981. (This text is now in its 3rd edn with various co-authors.)

Strategic Advertising Campaigns, Crain Books, 1979. Co author: Dennis G. Martin. (This text has been revised with various authors. It is now in its 5th edn with the 6th to be published, 2007.)

There are four Best Practice Benchmarking Studies conducted for the American Productivity and Quality Center, Houston. All resulted in bound books, all done with Heidi F. Schultz.

There are about 100 articles in various academic and professional journals. In addition, Schultz was the founding editor of the *Journal Of Direct Marketing* in the US. He has also been a monthly columnist for *Marketing News* (published by the American Marketing Association) for the last 10 years and an every-issue columnist for *Marketing Management*, (also published by the American Marketing Association) for the past five years.

9

....

Patricia Seybold

Customer experience expert

Patricia Seybold is founder and chief executive of the Patricia Seybold Group. With 28 years of experience consulting to customer-centric executives in technology-aggressive businesses across many industries, she has a special ability to spot the impact that technology enablement and customer behaviour will have on business trends very early.

She is thus able to provide Fortune 1000 companies with strategic insights, technology guidance and best practices. Her hands-on experience, her discovery and chronicling of best practices, her deep understanding of information technology, her large, loyal client base and her ongoing case study research enhances the thought leadership she offers.

She is also an internationally acclaimed best-selling author. Her book, Customers.com, *published in late 1998, provides insight into how 16 still-thriving companies designed their e-business strategies to improve revenues, increase profitability and enhance customer loyalty.* The Customer Revolution, *published in 2001, describes how 13 global businesses in a variety of industries were managed by and for customer value while they continuously improved the quality of the customer experience they delivered. She is co-author of* BrandChild, *published in 2003, which describes global tweens' and teens' relationship with brands. Her latest book,* Outside Innovation: How Your Customers Will Co-Design Your Company's Future, *describes customer-led innovation practices in 30 organizations. It was published in October 2006. Her books have been translated into over 10 languages.*

In addition to writing business bestsellers, Seybold has published dozens of research reports each year since the late 1970s. As publisher of Patricia Seybold Group's research and advisory services, she is responsible for setting the direction of the group's research agenda and is a frequent contributor of original research. She has authored numerous case studies for her research as well as for clients. Her work has also been published in the Harvard Business Review *and* Business 2.0, CIO Magazine, Fast Company, Computerworld, *and many other publications. She is frequently quoted in major publications such as* Business Week, *the* Wall Street Journal, *the* Financial Times, *the* New York Times, *and* Investor's Business Daily, *among others.*

The professional journey

Let's start with what you think you're best known for.

Sure. I think most people think of me in terms of customer experience and 'making it easier for customers to do business with you', which has been the phrase associated with me. It is based on the whole notion of designing your business around your customers – something that I've promulgated for many years.

When you started exploring these ideas, what was the wider context that made them seem relevant?

Well, there are actually two different threads of experiences. One was the overall information technology field – and I'm going back to, say, the mid-1980s. At that time our firm, a research and consulting firm, had as clients the people who were making purchasing decisions, not just about how much money to spend, but which products to buy to achieve the information technology visions for their organizations. Our client accounts were in many industries, everything from financial services to retail, manufacturers to publishers, and so on.

At that time, of course, computing was beginning to migrate from mainframe computers and minicomputers to PCs and networks. The internet hadn't yet hit. But even then, what our clients were telling us was, essentially, 'We've spent lots of money on technology and our customers still hate us, so we must be doing something wrong!' That was, if you like, the gauntlet that got thrown at me by several of my customers in the mid-1980s. They weren't saying that what we need is a customer relationship management (CRM) system. What they were basically saying was, 'Despite the money that we've spent on information technology, it doesn't seem to make our business any easier for our customers to interact with.'

So that was one of the calls to action. And then, by the mid-1990s as the internet began to move from research into commercial applications, and the web came along, and browser technology, I began to look much more closely at what was going on in e-commerce, which was the hot thing at that time. In other words, how do I do business on the web? How is business going to change because of the internet? Are stores going to go away? Will everybody shop online? Will intermediaries go away? Those were the kinds of questions that everybody was asking themselves.

In the mid-90s, many people were very confused about how to be successful with an internet strategy for their business. That was basically the environment in which I wrote *Customers.com*. After doing four years of research, from 1994 to 1998, I could see that the companies leading the way, like Cisco, Amazon and Wells Fargo, were all successful because they used the web to make it easy for customers to do business with them. So I kind of connected the dots between that first IT pain and what I saw actually working on the internet.

Did you have a background in technology?

No, my academic training was in comparative literature.

How did you make that transition?

When I graduated from college, I first became a school teacher and then worked in a bank in the systems department. Although I didn't have a computer background, because I was assistant to the head of operations, he showed me how to do the things he needed done. So my first exposure to programming was writing little routines and putting them on punched paper cards and then handing them in and getting my reports back.

Then I moved to Philadelphia in the mid-1970s, where my father, John Seybold, was. He had his own consulting and publishing firm and his clients were newspaper and magazine publishers.

I should say a bit about him. Starting in the 1960s, he was a pioneer in computer typesetting and put into commercial practice most of the concepts that are used now to create, edit, format and manipulate text information for print or electronic distribution. For example, he invented tagging, so that text could be reformatted in various ways, and then he invented computer programs to do that. That meta-tagging became SGML and then HTML. So he was very early in figuring how people were going to be interacting with information in a high level, meta-way.

By the time I arrived, the firm also had clients we called 'in-plant publishers', where companies like Caterpillar Tractor or John Hancock Insurance were using word processing systems with people in typing pools to produce things such as manuals and policies with in-house publishing systems. So that group became my clients and I quickly became a specialist in the word processing-to-publishing connection.

Then, one night in 1976 at the dinner table, I proposed that I create a variant of my father's very popular electronic publishing newsletter, *The Seybold Report*, and focus on word processing. So I started my own little division of the family company. And that led to my getting involved with word processing and later, office systems, professional computing, office computing and then on to the internet. And in the early 1980s, I spun my business out and moved to Boston, where I stayed as part of my father's company as a satellite office for a couple of years before I spun out completely on my own.

What was the business model you followed?

It was the one started by my father which I have continued for better or worse. It's a hybrid model. One part is based on a newsletter subscription model, based on research in the field, both with end users and suppliers, and the other is doing hands-on consulting work with both sets of parties – helping end users find and implement the right systems, and then helping suppliers develop the systems users actually want. The third leg of my father's model was the seminars that my father and brother started, Seybold Seminars, which my brother built up into the financial engine of the business before selling it off.

So would it be true to say that you learned about this area almost through osmosis rather than specific training?

That's absolutely true. I think apprenticeship is the best way to describe it. My father was taking me on consulting visits when I was still in my early twenties. He had a unique consulting approach which I picked up and have used ever since, based on his having been a labour arbitrator before becoming a business man. And that was to get all the key stakeholders around a table and start from there. You don't go and interview people individually and then write a report. You build a consensus about the issues and where you want to go. And I picked up the technology side by doing, as well as learning and listening.

Was the idea of 'customer focus' around when you were starting to build your career?

What was happening back in the mid- to late 1970s and early 1980s was end user focus. What I think distinguished our approach, both in the publishing world my dad started and then in the realm of the office that I got into, was that we always evaluated software applications from the standpoint of the people who would be using them.

Of course, other people were looking at functions and features, but nobody seemed to take the end user point of view the way we did. And maybe it was easier for us to do because we didn't have a computer background. I remember I would walk into a room at Digital or Wang and the people there would be really worried about what I was going to say. They would show me their latest products and I would say, 'Well, that's a bit awkward – why do it that way? It's not the way someone would really want to do it.' But a lot of times it was the programmers who had designed things without looking at the human factors.

Was it hard to get the message across that companies needed to think about users?

No, they were quite interested. There weren't that many human factors people around then. And I wasn't really a human factors specialist, but I was an end user advocate. Then I became, as I said, from the mid-1980s on, really, a customer advocate. But I've always kept the end user perspective as well.

So you were in there fairly early, and as it migrated to the idea of a customer as opposed to an end user?

Right.

And were you knocking on open doors as the years went by?

Generally speaking, yes. I've been very lucky that way. I've never had much difficulty getting people to listen to me or gaining entry. Back then I didn't always get invited into the executive suite, but I've always had a lot of credibility with the technical management and the business people who are technically savvy in companies. So that was our core focus originally and, now, it is increasingly the people who are the customer advocates.

What were some of the big challenges you have faced in getting your message across?

Well, my first book, *Customers.com*, was about making it easier for customers to do business with you through the internet. The second, *The Customer Revolution*, was a logical follow-on because it was all about making it easier for customers to do business with you across channels and touchpoints. It was really focusing on the customer experience, measuring and monitoring how well you are doing that and tying it back to your bottom line.

The truth is I've never had any trouble getting these messages across and appreciated in any organization. However, what happens is that in many organizations there is a degree of inertia, along with what I think of as immune systems and organizational structural issues, which make it very hard for companies to absorb, assimilate and take action. And you can come up with as many blueprints as you want – top-down leadership, customer champions, road maps for how to do things – but the fact of the matter is they're only going to work at the pace at which the organization's culture is able to absorb them.

That's not something that you can change overnight. It's really something that, no matter how well intentioned you are, no matter how customer-centric the top executives are, no matter how much good advice they get from outside consultants, no matter how visionary their internal executives are, we're talking about changing the human nervous system and behaviours, very ingrained behaviours. That takes three or four years. No matter how fast you want to move, human nature is going to get in the way. It's not about a particular type of person, because everybody usually has a lot of goodwill. It's trying to figure out what are really the best ways to get information flowing across these functional silos and to get everybody seeing things the same way. So those are the main challenges.

> *What happens is that in many organizations there is a degree of inertia . . . And you can come up with as many blueprints as you want – top-down leadership, customer champions, road maps for how to do things – but the fact of the matter is they're only going to work at the pace at which the organization's culture is able to absorb them.*

So three to four years is the average time it is going to take for a company to embrace this sort of customer-focused behaviour?

First of all, it's been my experience that things seem to take that long. And second, that three- to four-year number actually came from Fernando Flores (who is another guru I studied with for a while), who is an expert in cognitive learning. And he was the one who taught me that while you can learn to play tennis faster, you're not going to get masterful at tennis in less than three or four years. It takes a long time for the nervous system to replace itself; there's a lot of behaviour that is essentially wired in.

So is it essential that the drive to change comes from the top?

As I said, there are lots of blueprints and lots of different ways you can do it, and I've actually seen some pretty successful organizational transformations happen from the middle, up and down, or actually, probably better phrased, from the outside-in. Many of my clients happen to be the leaders in the e-business parts of the company. And many of them have, in fact, been the agents of transformation.

Why them, in your view?

Well, they are basically the ones who give customers the tools so that they can roll up their sleeves and start interacting with the business directly. And then, over time, customer pressure pushes all the way through the rest of the organization, both up and down. And eventually you see the tectonic plates shifting over time.

So, and this probably sounds quite obvious, it is technology that's been the catalyst?

I think technology has been the enabler – redesigning your company from the outside-in has been the catalyst. Because you can have websites and still not get any transformation; the only way you actually transform the culture is by being very thoughtful about who your customers are and what they're trying to do.

That has led to another subtle shift in the evolution of my own thinking. Back in the late 1990s and early 2000 I was known for the 'making it easier for customers to do business with you' concept. Over the last few years, I've actually been spending a lot of time with clients helping them go to the next step, which is not just making it easier for customers to do business with you, but making it easy for customers to do their jobs – to get things done.

Can you elaborate on that a bit?

I'll put it another way: 'making it easier for customers to accomplish their outcomes'. Helping customers get the stuff done they want to get done seems very prosaic, but it is the biggest challenge for marketing people, and actually for business people in general, because until you get there you can't do 'outside-in' transformation. You can make it easier for customers to place orders, but until you really can understand what it is they're trying to accomplish and how they're measuring their success, you haven't gone as far as you need to. Placing an order for something that you have is just a tiny part of their scenario. It's just an enabler for them to get something else done that they need to get done.

Do you think your message is getting through to the extent that, when you first started your journey, you hoped it would?

Well, I think certainly the 'make it easier for customers to do business with you' idea has taken off. It's got a complete life of its own. I'm delighted with that. But on the next level, I think that while everybody gets 'customer-centricity', theoretically, I don't think they quite understand how to do it.

The other idea that I have been talking about that is really taking off is improving the cross-channel customer experience. We need to make it seamless for customers as they interact with us across channels – through the web, phone or in the store, through retailers, distributors, field service – and so on. Offering a 'seamless customer experience' with your brand has now become a mantra. So again I find that gratifying. I don't have to preach that message anymore because everybody knows it.

But I think the other thing that I've been preaching and doing for 20 years that people still don't quite get, which I am hoping will somehow snap into place in the next year or so, is this idea that customers have things to do and we have to understand who the customers are, what they're motivated by and what it is they're trying to do. Then we just need to enable those 'Customer Scenarios®', streamline them and help customers transform them. It's so simple, but it's not part of any business strategy 101 book I've ever found.

Is that what your latest book is about?

It's certainly at the core of it. In *Outside Innovation*, I describe all the different ways that you can harness customers' creativity to help you redesign your business, your products and your business processes.

Current views of marketing

What, in your view, is the current state of marketing?

Well, there are two or three different variants of marketing I deal with. First, there are those rooted in the market research discipline, which I think is a little challenging because it's so data-driven and very hands-off.

I believe that in order to really understand your customers, you have to know who they are, what they care about and what they're trying to do. And that means you have to actually see them in the field. You have to do ethnographic research, and go watch them in their jobs and in their lives. You also, in my opinion, have to invite them in to co-design with you, co-design how they would ideally accomplish what they want to do, how they would *ideally* do what they want to do.

And that is the biggest obstacle that I'm running into right now. In most of the organizations I'm working with, the people in the marketing group, in the customer experience roles, in the e-business roles, are all very anxious to co-design with customers, with everything from getting them to help design new products, to getting them to help design their customer portals on their website, to helping them categorize their merchandise. These smart people know they need customers to help them with these things in order to get them right.

The problem is that a lot of times the market research group says, 'Oh, no, no, you can't actually invite customers to help you with that because you won't get an accurate statistical sample.' And so they end up going back to focus groups and surveys and statistics as opposed to ethnographic research and bringing in what I would call 'lead customers' to co-design with you. So I spend a lot of time with market researchers trying to convince them it's OK to actually bring customers in.

And the others?

There are plenty of marketing executives that are doing a great job. These are the people who are real-time data-driven from a marketing, merchandising and often internet perspective. They are the ones working on cross-sales and up-sales, merchandising and promotions, and typically in the online real-time world, doing things like search optimization.

In my opinion, most of these marketers are world class at being able to figure out that if a customer is thinking about buying a printer, then they probably also need to know about ink and toner and cables and computer connectivity and things like that. So they are looking at how customers are searching, what they want to see when they get there and what kind of cross-sales and up-sales they should be encouraging both on the site and by email marketing.

I think those people, who I call the interactive marketers, are superb. They really understand their customers, they understand the brand, they understand the experience and they're using data in a very 'real-time', interactive way to constantly up their conversion rates and the amount that each customer is buying, their lifetime value and so on. So I think we've made huge progress in that area.

And then there are the poor beleaguered customer experience folks.

Do you see more of people with that title? And why are they beleaguered?

Yes, it's happening a lot in the USA. It would be the vice president of customer experience or the director of customer experience or the customer experience officer. And usually they are in marketing. Sometimes it is the vice president of marketing who is the head of customer experience. And I wouldn't say it's very mature. I have probably a dozen clients with that title at this point.

It can be a difficult position because in most companies you're fighting organizational silos. Even though you may sit in marketing, obviously customer experience has a lot to do with customer support, as well as sales, operations, finance and accounting. It also includes retailers or third-party partners like value-added resellers, if you sell through them. They impact the customer experience a great deal. No matter how high you try to put these customer experience people in the organization, the fact of the matter is that most of the stuff that impacts the customer that they need to influence or ideally control is outside their purview.

So it depends on whether they're good enough to cut across functions?

Absolutely. They have to be somebody who is highly respected in the organization, who has been there forever, who's built a great network and has a lot of respect from all the other top executives. And then they have to lead by example and influence. There is certainly a lot of customer experience measurement that helps. Many companies now have customer loyalty scores, customer satisfaction, customer experience metrics of various kinds that are connected to executive and employee bonuses, compensation, and so that becomes their main – or one of their main – levers.

This doesn't seem to be marketing as we knew it but something new?

Yes, because customer experience is really a kind of hybrid: of e-business, marketing and then, ideally, customer support, product design, accounting and operations.

Surely some marketers won't be able to handle this?

I think they're all trying to get there. I think partly it depends on where marketing sits in the organization in terms of how much clout it has.

What other trends are you noticing in this field?

I see a big and a positive shift happening in terms of customer segmentation in two ways. One is that, in both consumer and business-to-business, I think people are beginning to understand that segmentation is very related to customer self-image and emotional motivations. So we're no longer just doing demographic segmentation. We're doing segmentation around, as I said, the emotional motivation and how somebody sees themselves. And to some extent certain companies, very brand-conscious companies, have always done that self-image segmentation. But in many other companies, particularly in business-to-business, that has never been done before, and so that's kind of new.

In the business-to-business world, by the way, that also often corresponds to job role segmentation, which is also new. People in business-to-business used to think simply in terms of 'I sell to Fortune 100 companies', 'I sell to mid-size companies'. Then they began to say, 'Oh, I sell to the "C" level, you know, chief marketing officer (CMO), the chief financial officer (CFO).' Well, neither of those approaches really works.

So now they are getting to the point where they say, 'I sell to enlightened IT managers' or 'I sell to hard-pressed accounting clerks'. They really have gotten to the point where they're thinking that the customer is somebody in a job with a particular emotional make-up or a self-image. And then they look at what those customers are trying to accomplish.

So, for example, in the USA, office supplies' retailer Staples has been very successful in the small business market by really understanding the people who buy office supplies in small businesses and just climbing right into their skin. And, if you understand them well enough, then you can work with them to redesign and transform how they do things. You then get this wonderful symbiotic effect and you can see it almost immediately on the bottom line.

Do you have any advice for marketers who want to excel in what could be called the age of the customer?

I think I have a few pieces of advice. One is to really engage with lead customers – the ones who are out in front and very passionate about things. Get them really hooked into your organization, and not just through surveys or user group meetings twice a year. One of the best practices that I've seen is when you actually build an online community of between 200 and 300 of your best customers. And you can recruit and incentivize them without spending much money. They love to be heard.

As one client said to me, 'It's like having all your customers in a conference room right down the hall. Any time you have any question about should we do it this way or that way you just open the door and ask them. And it's like – why wouldn't you do business that way?' So that is the challenge and something people should be doing.

One approach I've seen work well is for marketers to take particular customer segments and figure out what are the key scenarios for those customer segments – so, for each of those groups of customers, what are the two or three or four or five things that those people actually care about and are trying to do that intersect with your services and/or product? Then, ideally, bring people from different operational areas in your company together with that group of customers to co-design those customer scenarios. And what you get from that is this incredible kind of cross-functional shared mental model of 'Oh, here's how customers actually want to get things done, here's what we do today, here are the gaps, now let's see what we can do'.

Look at National Instruments, which is in my new book. This is a company that sells fairly esoteric software and hardware called 'virtual instrumentation' to engineers and scientists in hundreds of different disciplines. While the company is 30 years old, this particular software platform has been around for 20 years and in that time the company has built the most vibrant customer communities. About 50% of all new products are actually either created by customers or created as a direct response to customers' needs. And then customers do most of the customer support for each other. Customers develop extensions and applications and put them back into the community. So it's a great example of a company where customers really are at the core.

And everybody in the organization tells stories. So that's another core competency that I think that marketing people really need to get good at. Many of our clients are asking for help with stories. At National Instruments, in every meeting, somebody will tell a

Really engage with lead customers – the ones who are out in front and very passionate about things. Get them really hooked into your organization, and not just through surveys or user group meetings twice a year. And you can recruit and incentivize them without spending much money. They love to be heard.

story about some new, clever way a customer has used its technology. All of the employees in the company are just endlessly curious about what customers are trying to do and how they're using their technology to do it and what else they need.

And the other piece of advice?

I believe that marketing and customer support shouldn't be two separate organizations reporting typically to two separate chains of command. That's got to go away because really it's just inhibiting the ability to deliver good customer experience.

And do you recommend this when you go in to your clients?

I do, and I find it very difficult to get anybody to take me up on it because it's just very ingrained. We've got sales, we've got marketing and we've got support. Everybody thinks that that is the customer life cycle. It isn't. The customer life cycle starts with planning and decision-making and it goes all the way through repurchase or whatever. Most organizations just have those very awkwardly segmented. I think that will begin to change over the next few years.

Getting more personal

What is it about you, do you think, that has got you to where you are now?

I think the fact that I am actually very interested in and curious about what it is people care about and how they go about solving problems. So my favourite activity is to interview customers, talk to them about what they're trying to do, how they're going about doing it or how they did this project or initiative they have just finished.

And has the fact that you obviously come from a very impressive family been an influence at all?

Well, I think it's helped. Also, I grew up in a college town so I've always had a lot of intellectual stimulation. My parents always made sure to bring interesting people around. We had great dinner table conversations.

Was it a bit challenging as well?

I never felt that I was competing for mind share or market share or whatever. I've actually enjoyed the fact that I've got this great Seybold brand that I've been able to ride on, even after I eventually went out on my own.

Do you have what you consider a defining moment in your life?

For me it was probably when I was 18 and in religious studies class in college and read about Pierre Teilhard de Chardin and the 'Noosphere'. That was obviously way before the internet and before I was the least bit interested in computers. But there was this sudden epiphany when I realized that this whole idea of a mantle of shared human knowledge and spirituality surrounding the globe was something that was going to be enabled in my lifetime and that I was going to be involved in.

My defining moment was probably when I was 18 and in religious studies class in college and read about Pierre Teilhard de Chardin and the 'Noosphere'. That was obviously way before the internet and before I was the least bit interested in computers. But there was this sudden epiphany when I realized that this whole idea of a mantle of shared human knowledge and spirituality surrounding the globe was something that was going to be enabled in my lifetime and that I was going to be involved in.

You must be proud of many things, but is there anything in particular you could mention?

Actually I think I'm probably proudest of my lifestyle. A lot of people are proud of external accomplishments or the amount of money they've made or the amount of fame or whatever.

Do tell us more.

So at this moment I'm sitting in my farmhouse up in Maine on the water. I spend four days a week here, usually from Thursday nights to Monday nights, sometimes even up to a couple of weeks. I'm here with my dog and my cat and I walk in the woods and poke around in the garden and basically I'm able to be reflective. Now, it doesn't mean I'm not emailing clients or having phone meetings with them, but it's a great balance. And then other times I'm down in my office in Boston having meetings there. Or else I'll be visiting with clients, out doing research or making speeches.

I guess that's the other thing I'm proudest of. I have set up my life and my business so that I have complete control over my time.

Selected publications

Books

Outside Innovation: How Your Customers Will Co-Design Your Company's Future, Collins, 2006.

BrandChild: Insights into the Minds of Today's Global Kids: Understanding their Relationship with Brands, Kogan Page, 2003. Co-author: Martin Lindstrom.

The Customer Revolution, Crown Business, 2001. Co-author: Ronni T. Marshak.

Customers.com: How to Create a Profitable Business Strategy for the Internet and Beyond, Crown Business, 1998. Co-author: Ronni T. Marshak.

Articles

'A Call for Accounting Transparency: The Value of Customers and Brands, New Rules for Disclosing Intangible Assets Will Require Reporting on Customer and Brand Assets', Patricia Seybold Group, Inc., 2005.

'Customer-Led Innovation Spawns Mergers', Patricia Seybold Group, Inc., 2005.

'Customer Portals: Central to Your Customer Experience Strategy, Customer Portals Support Your Customers throughout Their Lifecycles', Patricia Seybold Group, Inc., 2005.

'Design Your Quality of Customer Experience (QCE)^{SM} Scorecard, Create a Small, Focused Set of Metrics; Measure What Matters to Your Customers', Patricia Seybold Group, Inc., 2005.

'Establishing and Nurturing a Customer-Centric Culture: Lessons Learned from the Masters (Caterpillar Financial Services, Harrah's Entertainment, and Lands' End)', Patricia Seybold Group, Inc., May 2005.

'How Should You Manage Customer and Partner Portals?, Patty's Dream Team: Roles and Responsibilities You'll Need for Your Customer-Centric Organization', Patricia Seybold Group, Inc., 2005.

'How to Think about Content Management, Confused about Content Management and Portals? Reframe Your Questions', Patricia Seybold Group, Inc., 2005.

'Let Customers Co-Design Your Customer-Critical Initiatives: How and When to Use Customer Scenario® Mapping', Patricia Seybold Group, Inc., 2005.

'Let Customers Co-Design Your Customer-Critical Initiatives: Why and When to Use Customer Scenario® Mapping', Patricia Seybold Group, Inc., May 2005.

'Nurturing Customer Loyalty in the B2B World: Know and Nurture Your Internal Advocates', Patricia Seybold Group, Inc., 2005.

'Partner Portals Should be Combined with Customer Portals: Why Not Design Your Partner Portals to Surround and Complement Your Customer Portals?', Patricia Seybold Group, Inc., 2005.

'What Are Customer Experience Best Practices? Summary of Our Findings from the APQC Total Customer Experience Benchmark and a Report Card for You', Patricia Seybold Group, Inc., 2005.

'Best Practices in Dealing with Consumers' Cross-Channel Retail Behavior: Meeting Consumers' "Moments of Truth" as They Shop across Channels', Patricia Seybold Group, Inc., 2004.

'Customer (and Partner) Segment Advocates, Patty's Dream Team: Roles and Responsibilities You'll Need for Your Customer-Centric Organization', Patricia Seybold Group, Inc., 2004.

'Key Role: SVP of Cross-Channel Customer Experience (or Equivalent), Patty's Dream Team: Roles and Responsibilities You'll Need for Your Customer-Centric Organization', Patricia Seybold Group, Inc., 2004.

'Looking for Business Architects? Check Out Your E-business Leader', Patricia Seybold Group, Inc., 2004.

'Rethinking CRM: Customers Don't Want to Be Managed; They Do Want Good Experiences and Outcomes', Patricia Seybold Group, Inc., 2004.

'Sr. IT Architect for Cross-Channel Customer Experience, Patty's Dream Team: Roles and Responsibilities You'll Need for Your Customer-Centric Organization', Patricia Seybold Group, Inc., 2004.

'VP of Customer Intelligence, Patty's Dream Team: Roles and Responsibilities You'll Need for your Customer-Centric Organization', Patricia Seybold Group, Inc., 2004.

'Where Does Support Fit in Your Customers' Lifecycles? Everywhere! Support Isn't a Stage in the Customer Lifecycle; It's the Engine That Drives it!', Patricia Seybold Group, Inc., 2004.

'Why It's Hard to Prioritize IT Initiatives around End-Customer Impacting Issues: Current Disconnects between Business and IT; Suggestions for Bridging the Gaps', Patricia Seybold Group, Inc., 2004.

'Beware of Business Process Management, Be Careful about Adopting Internally-Driven Business Processes; Instead, Design a Customer-Adaptive Enterprise Using a Services-Oriented Approach', Patricia Seybold Group, Inc., 2003.

'Gathering Customers' Real Requirements: Uncovering Customers' Moments of Truth', Patricia Seybold Group, Inc., 2003.

'How Should You Manage Content within Your Enterprise? Seven Key Issues that Are Critical to Success', Patricia Seybold Group, Inc., 2003.

'Netflix.com Wins Patent on Business Methods: Turning Customers' "Moments of Truth" into a Sustainable, Competitive Advantage', Patricia Seybold Group, Inc., July 2003.

'Support for Business Processes (Theirs and Ours): Your Customers' Scenarios Drive; Your Business Processes Support', Patricia Seybold Group, Inc., 2003.

'Wanted: Information Architects! Improving the Findability of Enterprise Information', Patricia Seybold Group, Inc., 2003.

'Get Inside the Lives of Your Customers', *Harvard Business Review*, May 2001.

10

....

Jack Trout

Positioning pioneer

Jack Trout is president of Trout & Partners, a prestigious marketing firm with headquarters in Old Greenwich, Connecticut, USA, and offices in 13 countries. Instrumental in developing the vital approach to marketing known as 'positioning', he is responsible for some of the freshest ideas to be introduced into marketing thinking in the last several decades.

Trout manages and supervises a global network of experts that apply his concepts and develop his methodology around the world. The firm has done work for AT&T, IBM, Burger King, Merrill Lynch, Xerox, Merck, Lotus, Ericsson, Tetra Pak, Repsol, Hewlett-Packard, Procter & Gamble, Southwest Airlines and other Fortune 500 companies.

He started his business career in the advertising department of General Electric (GE). From there he went on to become a divisional advertising manager at Uniroyal. Then he joined Al Ries in the advertising agency and marketing strategy firm where they worked together for over 26 years.

He co-authored the industry classic, Positioning: The Battle for Your Mind, *with Ries, which was published in 1980. In 1985 he and Ries wrote a second bestselling book entitled* Marketing Warfare. Positioning *and* Marketing Warfare *are now published in 14 languages. In 1988* Bottom-Up-Marketing *was published. In 1993 their book,* The 22 Immutable Laws of Marketing *became a marketing bible. It outlined the basic reasons why marketing programs succeed or fail in the competitive 1990s.*

Trout closed the circle with the sequel to Positioning *in 1995. Entitled* The New Positioning, *it takes one of the world's foremost business strategies to a new level. It became a* Business Week *bestseller and has already been translated into 16 languages. This was followed by* The Power of Simplicity – A Management Guide to Cutting through the Nonsense and Doing Things Right. *In 2001 he wrote* Differentiate or Die – Survival in Our Era of Killer Competition *which presented the keys to survival in a killer global economy. This has also become a bestseller.*

The professional journey

Where did the idea of positioning come from?

Well, we're going back a long time here so remembering is a little tricky. It was 1969; I had joined Al Ries in an advertising agency and was looking for a way to represent how we approached problems to differentiate our agency from others.

Essentially, what struck me was that we tended to approach problems from a very strategic point of view. Basically, you start with the competition. I realized that defining positioning – taking the word to describe how we set up our clients' products in the mind of the customers and vis-à-vis the competition – is where it all starts.

So, I wrote a one-page memo to Al and said that I thought we could represent our thought processes, the way we deal with problems, by what I called 'positioning'.

That's how we started to separate our thinking in a unique way from that of other agencies. As for the reason I wanted to do it this way, well most advertising agencies – even to this day – like to lay claim to creativity. I said, 'No, let's not do that, let's focus on strategy and positioning.' So that's what we did.

What was his reaction?

He looked at my memo and said, 'This is very good. I think there might be something here.' He suggested that I wrote an article, which was published in *Industrial Marketing* magazine in 1969. Then I wrote another in 1971. The articles, even though I was out of the marketing mainstream as such, started to generate interest and momentum.

A year later, Al and I co-authored a series in *Advertising Age*, a three-parter. This is what set us on the road to fame. What started out as just a way to separate out our thinking from that of other agencies turned into a real strategic concept. It focused on how the mind works, how it takes in information and stores it. In a way we just sort of backed into this concept, which eventually ran around the world and in 1980 we published a book. The rest is history, but that was its genesis.

How much of that was helped by your background on the client side as well?

A lot, I think. You know I started at GE, as did Al, and when you start at a company like that (which had a big fancy training program in those days), you're obviously going to be very well grounded in competition and strategy – much more so than working in advertising. That industry is much more about ads, about being clever and cute.

When you start to write advertising copy to sell your ideas within a company – and that is what you are doing all the time in that world – you have to be very well grounded.

Does that mean positioning is rooted in strategy?

Let me tell you a funny real-life story. I was making one of my strategy presentations at a GE analysis session. I had a flip chart presentation, showing the strategy (I think it was the motor business). I'll never forget this marketing guy, probably twice my age, staring out the window while I'm doing my flip chart. This made me very uncomfortable.

He looked back, noticed my discomfort and said, 'Look kid, put aside your presentation. I want to give you some facts of life here at GE. The problem isn't out there in the marketplace. We are GE, we do motors, come on. The problem, to be honest with you, is in this building. Give me a flip chart that gets everybody in this building pointed in the same direction, and then we can flatten anything out there.'

I use that story endlessly as I travel around company after company because that is often the problem. How do you get everybody inside the building focused on a strategy that you are taking out into the marketplace? It's a gigantic problem in many big companies and corporations. I've even discovered it's the same when I've been doing work in recent years for the State Department. How do we build brand America? I've been working recently for the Democrats versus the Republicans. How do we position them? You just can't imagine the difficulties of trying to do this in Washington.

So, in a way, I have discovered that this is a universal problem. That's really what positioning is all about, it's that starting point. What is our strategy? What is the idea we want to stick in the minds? So that's how it all began.

What spread the word about positioning?

The thing that really spread the word was the *Ad Age* series. Reprints of them went all around the world. That seeded the concept in people's minds and gave it momentum.

Which people within organizations were keenest to take you up on what you were talking about and who offered the most resistance?

In the early years, we had a lot of resistance from other advertising people. They said, 'That's not going to happen. Who are these people saying that this is the next big thing?' The arguments dissipated fairly quickly, though.

Marketing people within companies were the first to begin to embrace this body of work. The chief executive officer (CEO) level was always difficult to reach unless you were in smaller companies. I have the most fun when I'm dealing with entrepreneurs, the guys that are really involved with it. But when you're dealing with the AT&Ts, the IBMs, you just have a hard time working your way to the top. The biggest problem has been that CEOs are not involved.

I remember giving a big presentation at IBM on our strategy. A young lady came up and said, 'The chat was very good but it'll never happen here.' I asked why and she replied: 'You don't have the right people in the room. They don't come to these meetings. Your idea won't survive because everybody's got an agenda here.'

That's equally true, as I discovered recently, in Washington. I was told: 'Jack, that strategy you developed for the Democrats is terrific but you are violating the law of the meeting. In Washington,' the guy went on, 'you have to go to all the meetings, because everybody has their own agenda. Unfortunately, you don't go to all the meetings because you are not an insider. So forget it. It's not going to happen.' I've discovered that over and over again.

Who, in those early days, were the main influences on your work?

We had our heroes. Ultimately, one of my main sources of inspiration was David Ogilvy. In many ways he thought like we did, was very strategic, very rational, had this direct response mentality and wasn't a creativity guy. Bill Bernbach was the creativity guy, although he was very strategic in his approach.

So we looked to the giants of that moment – Ogilvy, Bernbach and to some degree Leo Burnett – but the great irony is that there are no giants anymore.

If you were trying to spread the word about positioning now for the first time, as a completely new concept, would it be as relevant?

I think that, as the years roll by, we've discovered that positioning and marketing warfare have become more important. These books keep selling and the reason is that the level of competition is increasing. Remember, all of our work essentially starts with competition.

How do you position yourself against competitors? Who owns what idea? Who doesn't? In marketing warfare we say, 'How do you deal with that? Here are the ground rules. And then, how do you differentiate yourselves from the competition?'

All of our work revolves around how you cope with competition. I'm always asked, 'What has changed in all the years that you have been doing this stuff?' and I say, 'Here's what's changed – the level of competition.'

We wrote *Marketing Warfare* some 20 years ago, and *Positioning* some five years earlier. We wrote that this is the game you play in today's market. In fact, the opening article I wrote was 'Positioning – The Game People Play in Today's Me-Too Marketplace'. So, in other words, the first article, back in 1969, talked about the me-too marketplace, the competitive marketplace.

Now, I didn't realize it then, but that was a tea party. Today, it's a me-too marketplace because you've got competition coming at you from absolutely every angle, from all over the world. So in a way, the body of work that we've done is probably even more important today than it was then, because the level of competition is more intense today.

> *I think that, as the years roll by, we've discovered that positioning and marketing warfare become more important. These books keep selling and the reason is the level of competition is increasing. Remember, all of our work essentially starts with competition. How do you position yourself against competitors? Who owns what idea? Who doesn't? In marketing warfare we say, 'How do you deal with that? Here are the ground rules. And then, how do you differentiate yourselves from the competition?'*

What issues are you looking at in your latest book on strategy?

The latest book addresses the problem I discussed earlier. In other words, I consider the biggest problem facing marketing today is Wall Street and the lack of involvement of top people, the CEOs. If you can't get them involved, if you don't have the right people in the room, it's a gigantic problem.

I said to myself, 'I'm going to write a book which essentially is everything I have written on strategy over the last 25 years.' It's a summation book that takes about three hours to read and is written for CEOs. I said, 'Look, I'm going to bring these guys up to speed in three hours. I'll give them a sense of what marketing and strategy is all about.'

It starts with positioning, goes into marketing warfare and then into differentiation and so on. It's trying to say, 'Look, guys, this is the one book to read if you're reading only one.'

Have you noticed in your many travels any difference in the way these ideas are is viewed in different parts of the world?

What I discovered is that it varies, by region and area. In marketing terms, the USA is probably a little bit more sophisticated in many ways because we've been at it for such a long time. We've had maybe 25 years of intense competition and I think the more competition you have, the more you have to get good at this stuff, at marketing strategy, or you get killed. So maybe, because of the level of competition here, we're a little more advanced.

Western Europe isn't bad, although Spain is still the old boy network. It's so interesting. It's who you know and what your politics are. You go to Germany and they're kind of stubborn, still very driven by the old boys, not easy to get them to change. The Scandinavians, in contrast, are very advanced, very good, because they've always been a trading nation.

Russia is also getting into marketing. I've been there a number of times recently. I'm treated sort of like a marketing rock star because of my books. Are they really good at it? Not really yet. They don't have much to sell. They're still pretty much driven by minerals and petroleum. But they are getting into it.

I am even beginning to see a lot of interest in marketing in places like the Ukraine. Everybody is trying to get in on the game because of the global economy. In other words, they have got to figure out how to play.

Asia is a whole other world. China is really getting into marketing with a vengeance. The Chinese are amazing. They are very open to taking in Western ideas as to what to do, looking for new ways of marketing and trying to learn. Japan, on the other hand, is very difficult because the Japanese can't stand to have anybody tell them how to run their business if you're not Japanese. The Japanese are really good at manufacturing and technology but very bad at marketing. They are very closed-minded.

Current views of marketing

You've said that the marketing industry nowadays lacks giants. Why is that?

They're all gone. There is nobody who is essentially developing theories, ideas, approaches. It's just a bunch of financial guys. That is one of the problems in the ad business. Now, that is the opposite of the founders of the agency business. They were very much involved with the strategy.

Here's a great story. Many years ago I was with a senior account guy, much older than me, who told me a story. He said, 'Jack, let me tell you what's happened. When I was doing a trade show for one of our clients, the head of the agency was lying on the bed with the CEO of this big client in a hotel room at the show. They were discussing strategy, and the CEO was saying, "Well, I think we should do such and such", while Ray was saying, "No, no, you're wrong, this is what we should do."' After he told me the tale he said, 'Jack, that is the problem. We're not in bed with our clients anymore.'

And he's right. That is what has happened. I mean if you were an Ogilvy or a Bernbach, you could sit down with a client and discuss strategy, what you should and shouldn't do. Nowadays the financial guys who run the big agencies can't do that. Are you kidding? So here's the issue – advertising firms should be like law firms They shouldn't have gone public, they shouldn't be like their own clients. That's the problem.

Is that changing?

I think it's beginning to. We are seeing the return of the smaller agencies, where the top management people are now involved with the problems. You're beginning to see a lot of the big clients saying, 'You know what? I think a lot of the big monolithic agencies are just out to help themselves.' So, they're starting to break up their accounts and give a piece of business to the smaller shops, where once again the senior people at the agencies are doing the work. You can't have kids doing this stuff.

What about the perception of marketing and the esteem in which marketers are held?

The perception of marketers is not good. Marketing itself is in a bit of a crisis mode right now. You are seeing a lot of folks who are unsure what to do: 'Should I advertise? Should I go into the brave new world of online?' There's a lot of confusion right now.

You're also seeing a lot of categories sliding into commodities. This is a big mistake. There is enormous power resting with top retailers like Wal-Mart. So marketers, in a way, are losing some credibility. Then too, even though you see new job titles like chief marketing officer (CMO) spring up, these guys don't last as long as National Football League coaches. I mean, these guys are out in a heartbeat.

Marketers are always complaining that they are not taken seriously enough by those at the top. How do they overcome that?

You really have to involve the top management guys in the strategy of what you are doing. You have to force them into it and they have to understand what you are doing and why – and why you're spending money on it. And sometimes, people don't do that very well.

You have to be willing to put it right out on the table and say: 'Ladies and gentlemen, this is what we've got to do as a company. This is our strategy and if you do that we won't be.able to do this.' And they have to fight for these things, because everybody has agendas.

Remember, the guy who has the ear of the CEO today is the chief financial officer. He's the one running the numbers, dealing with Wall Street and as long as Wall Street is the big factor out there, it is very difficult for marketers.

> *You really have to involve the top management guys in the strategy of what you are doing. You have to force them into it and they have to understand what you are doing and why – and why you're spending money on it. And sometimes, people don't do that very well. You have to be willing to put it right out on the table and say: 'Ladies and gentlemen, this is what we've got to do as a company. This is our strategy and if you do that we won't be able to do this.'*

Can you elaborate?

The problem is growth at all cost. Wall Street, the financial community, wants to see how much you are going to grow, quarter by quarter. If it doesn't see that you're on a growth path, it will savage your stock. This terrifies all the guys who are pushing their stock.

Really, you have to introduce what I call the Warren Buffett (the great investor and head of Berkshire Hathaway) school of marketing. You have to ask yourself, 'How do I build a business?' You can't worry about your stock. If you get a company hooked on stock prices you've got an Enron problem, because people will do anything to keep their stock up. That is the road to rack and ruin.

You really have to say, 'No, I am in the business of selling widgets and I'm going to work on that. I don't care what you guys think, I'm going to approach this thing from what's best from my business point of view, and if things work out, my stock will be OK.' But you cannot get sucked into the Wall Street game.

That presumably applies to all types of companies: clients, agencies, manufacturing companies, retail?

That's exactly right. Pressure from the stock market forces you to do things that are just not very smart. Once I was asked in by a big drug company to sit in on its meeting on marketing plans. One of the young marketing guys stood up and said, 'Next year we will be facing a very big new competitor and it's going to be tough. So here are my numbers.'

He was predicting 15% growth. So I said, 'Wait a minute. You just told me that you have new competition. I would have been impressed if you were going to break even or stay the same. But 15%? Well, how are you going to do that?

And he replied, 'Well, don't ask me, ask my boss. He made me put that number in there.'

So, I go to his boss, and say, 'This isn't real.'

And he says, 'Don't tell me. I got a problem with *my* boss.'

And his boss is the CEO of a public company and he wants 15% growth. That's what I mean. It forces unreality into a marketing strategy, and that's how line extensions and all this stuff have come from 'How do I keep growing?'

If this pressure continues, what do you see happening in the future?

You are going to have a lot of companies in trouble because nastiness happens. The marketplace is very tough right now, and here's your problem: if you make a mistake and lose your business, you don't get it back. And that is what happened at General Motors (GM).

It's a classic example of what I'm talking about. GM did it across all its brands. 'Chevrolet? How do I make more money? OK, I'll have expensive Chevrolets and cheap Chevrolets. Buicks? I'll have cheap Buicks and expensive Buicks.'

They make everything for everybody and guess what: now its brands are in very bad shape, as is the company. It might have got away with it when there was no competition, but now it has the Japanese, the Koreans and the Germans. In other words, you make a mistake in today's competitive world, you get killed.

Which company, by contrast, would you say has got it right?

Let's take Toyota. It has a very powerful differentiating idea, of reliability. It's perceived to be an incredibly reliable car. And it delivers. It will give you reliability and in a limited number of forms. You have the Corollas, the Avalons – a family of cars, but they're all reliable and, just as BMW will give you driving machines, Toyota gives you that 'drivability' idea. Companies like that stay within set limits, yet at the same time, they are very good at turning out a new idea.

You said before that you believed the Japanese were not very good at marketing, but excellent at manufacturing. Are companies like Toyota and Honda exceptions to the rule because they seem to be good at both?

Honda isn't bad, but I would say that Toyota is the real exception. There are too many Hondas. They get into stuff like motor bikes, home generators, mowers and so on, so I don't give them high marks because they line extend like crazy. But not Toyota. And when it went upmarket, it went to the Lexus. So Toyota is the best, even though it's an anomaly. I don't consider Honda anywhere near its level.

Sony's problem, meanwhile, was it got into too much stuff. It shouldn't have bought a movie studio, all that kind of craziness, that's what hurt. What did it do next? It came out with the Walkman, but the next generation – the digital version – went to Apple with its iPods. The same sort of thing happened with Sony's flat big wide screen televisions. It hasn't done well because it never stayed focused enough.

Are there any marketing myths that you would like to eliminate?

Well, we've been railing about line extensions, trying to take one brand and make it represent many things, instead of staying focused on one thing and one idea and staying with it. But again, what pushes companies off that is Wall Street. 'How do I grow, how do I get bigger?' The other thing that we talk about (and I'm supposed to be writing a book on) is specialization.

This is an important issue, because it's counter to growth and getting big. Specialization is about being very very good at one thing and then owning it in the mind of your customers. Trust me, that is your best defence against competition.

Can you give us an example?

I'll give you the ultimate example. There is a small firm in the middle of England somewhere called Martin-Baker. It makes a Martin-Baker ejection seat for military aircraft. This is *the* ejection seat that every military aircraft has to have. I got to see a film of a demo when I was in naval aviation.

When was this?

This was back in the late 1950s or early 1960s. Now, that company is still sitting there in the middle of England making ejection seats and they're the best. It is the generic specialist in ejection seats. I suspect that you could talk to anyone building a fighter aircraft anywhere in the world and they would want a Martin-Baker ejection seat.

What companies would you look to in the USA?

Let's look to United Technologies Corporation (UTC). It's very big and very successful but, guess what? It's big because it has a portfolio of specialists: Carrier Air Conditioning, Otis Elevators (the king of elevators), Pratt & Whitney aircraft engines, Sikorsky Aircraft Corporation. In other words, what they have built is very powerful portfolio of specialists who are brilliant in the one thing they do.

Even though they are part of a much larger company, they operate pretty much as big specialists and are well focused. So I think that, in the future, if you are not really very good at one thing – the Harvard people would call it 'core competency' – the biggest mistake in marketing is trying to be everything to everybody, which gets you into the line extensions. And that is the greatest problem in the world of marketing.

And you know why? You can't do that anymore, there's too much competition. In the old days you could get away with it, not any more.

So, presumably when we're talking about the biggest challenge, it's not to diversify too much?

That is exactly right. And if you are going play a diversified game, you have to play it the way United Technologies played it; you have to have a portfolio of specialists. Very few people, if you were to ask them, would know who owns Otis. They'd say, 'Otis is an elevator company.' They'd have no idea that it's UTC. Because the only people who really care are Wall Street. That's the stock they buy. But UTC is kept totally out of the marketing. It is purely a financial holding.

How big an impact is technology having?

Technology is a big factor because it pushes new generations of products into the game. Technology is how you innovate.

Peter Drucker had it perfectly way, way back. Most people have forgotten this. He said that a company's role is to produce new customers and there are only two internal functions that do so. One is marketing and the other innovation. Every other function in a company is subordinate to that. He is absolutely correct. It is marketing and innovation, and technology is generally what drives the innovation.

What should companies be doing in this incredibly challenging climate?

The biggest thing that they have to understand is, I think, differentiation. It's the title of one of my books, *Differentiate or Die*. Your assignment is to find a way to separate yourself from your competition in a meaningful way, and marketers have to build a program around that point of difference.

If it's Toyota, it's reliability. If it's BMW, it's the driving machine. If it's Volvo, it's safety. You have to have a point of differentiation that you can nurture, and be able to convince your top management that this is it. You can't let them force you to do things, where an idea falls apart because you are into too many variations.

You know, Coca-Cola was the real thing once upon a time. It invented the cola business. That was its idea, and it should never have abandoned it. That means you can't have all these other things, all these variations on variations. So for me, the marketer today has to really understand the power of differentiation.

When you go to companies, what's the reaction to your telling them these uncomfortable truths about what they need to do?

When I show up at a place, normally it's to help overcome a big problem. So I end up riding into town like a gunfighter, and my first task is to shoot a few people, shoot a few ideas. That is what I've got to do to clean up the town.

I'm brutally honest. I say, 'What did you do that for? That doesn't make any sense.' Or I say, 'I'm not liking this.' When I say that to the people in the room, a lot of people get uncomfortable, very uncomfortable.

Do they listen?

Well, they listen while I'm there, and then I say, 'This is what you're going to do now I've got the town organized. Right? See you!' Then I ride out of town. That's when some of those guys come out from behind the bushes asking whether I've gone. And they go right back to doing what they were doing before, or they try to, unless the CEO, or the senior guys, say, 'No – you heard what Jack said.' If no one does that, forget it.

That is the way it works, believe me. It is the life of the gunfighter and the thing is, I love it, because I've got the fastest gun, and no one in a meeting room is going to outshoot me. And usually they are too afraid to shoot. They never even go for their gun. They'll just hide out and wait till I leave.

Getting more personal

What do you feel are the personal qualities that have enabled you to excel in this area?

In my case I would say it's my ability to be a quick study. In other words, it's the gunfighter simile again. You have to be very quick, because when you walk into a room, you don't have a lot of time. Everyone is staring at you and you have to come up with the solution. So you have to be a quick study. You cannot just be methodical, and you have to be able to conceptualize. So it is conceptualizing and the ability to do it quickly that's key to doing my kind of business, why I'm good at what I do.

Was there a defining moment in your career?

Well, I would say the defining moment was probably when I cooked up positioning. That was really the defining moment.

Has the message from your ideas got through to the extent that you thought it would or hoped it would?

I guess the answer is yes and no. I get many people sending me emails or meeting me in the street who say: 'Oh Jack, I read your book and did it. It's terrific and it worked.' In fact, I got an email from a stonemason, in North Carolina. He said, 'I read your books and I figured it all out. I now only do decorative masonry, and am very successful. And I just sold my company for $25 million!' And I just get $19.95 for the book and that's it!

Has it gotten through everywhere? Well, at AT&T I was there at a critical juncture trying to get it to pursue the right strategy. I couldn't get it to do it and AT&T was absorbed by one of the Baby Bells, although the name

> *I get many people sending me emails or meeting me in the street who say: 'Oh Jack, I read your book and did it. It's terrific and it worked.' In fact, I got an email from a stonemason, in North Carolina. He said, 'I read your books and I figured it all out. I now only do decorative masonry, and am very successful. And I just sold my company for $25 million!' And I just get $19.95 for the book and that's it!*

has now been resurrected. With many companies it was a case of working it up to the CEO and management, trying to get them off of the Wall Street trap. So it's a mixed success out there in a very difficult world.

Selected publications

Jack Trout on Strategy, McGraw-Hill, March 2004.

A Genie's Wisdom: A Fable of How a CEO Learned to Be a Marketing Genius, John Wiley & Sons, Inc., November 2002.

Big Brands, Big Trouble: Lessons Learned the Hard Way, John Wiley & Sons, Inc., 2001.

Positioning: The Battle for Your Mind. 20th anniversary edn, McGraw-Hill, December 2000. Co-author: Al Ries.

Differentiate or Die, John Wiley & Sons, Inc., 2000. Co-author: Steve Rivkin.

The Power of Simplicity, McGraw-Hill, November 1998. Co-author: Steve Rivkin.

The New Positioning, McGraw-Hill, 1996. Co-author: Steve Rivkin.

The 22 Immutable Laws of Marketing, HarperCollins, 1993. Co-author: Al Ries.

Bottom-Up Marketing, McGraw-Hill, 1989. Co-author: Al Ries.

Marketing Warfare, McGraw-Hill, 1986. Co-author: Al Ries.

Positioning: The Battle for Your Mind, McGraw-Hill, 1981. Co-author: Al Ries.

11

....

Lester Wunderman

Direct marketing missionary

Lester Wunderman, the founder of Wunderman and widely acknowledged as the 'father' of direct marketing, spawned an entirely new way of selling products and services. Hired as a copywriter at Maxwell Sackheim & Co. in 1947, Wunderman blossomed as a strategist. Recognizing that many 'mail order' accounts were ripe for growth through broader marketing efforts, he introduced his 'direct marketing' concept. He established Wunderman, Ricotta & Kline in 1958 (acquired by Young & Rubicam in 1973) and, with his vast multimedia agency, created direct-selling breakthrough campaigns, which built the Columbia Record Club and the American Express travel and entertainment credit card businesses.

He has received many awards and tributes from both the direct marketing and general advertising industries, including being named to the Direct Marketing Hall of Fame in 1983. In 1998, he was elected to the Advertising Hall of Fame and was named as one of 20 'Advertising Legends and Leaders' by Adweek Magazine.

In addition to his role as Chairman Emeritus at Wunderman, he also currently serves as Director of i-Behavior, a premier provider of database targeting services. His book Being Direct: Making Advertising Pay *was first published in 1996, and his highly respected collection of Dogon art is part of the permanent collection of New York's Metropolitan Museum of Art.*

The professional journey

What do you feel you're best known for, given the span of your career?

That's a good question. I hadn't thought of it, but I think if I were to be known for anything, it would be the encouragement of a dialogue between the consumer and the advertiser. Historically, it was the advertiser with the power of speech and the consumer who listened.

The exception, I suppose, was in the earliest days when dialogue existed in the physical marketplace. But dialogue disappeared with media. The media initiated one-way speech: advertisers would say what their product was and describe its benefits, while the consumer had no choice other than to listen. I think the miracle of today's marketing is the ability of the consumer to both listen and speak, plus the ongoing and increasing informed dialogue.

This informed dialogue between the advertiser and the consumer entails not only the consumer knowing what the advertiser is saying or has said but, increasingly, the advertiser knowing who the consumer is and, to some degree, what they have done and what they are likely to be doing in the future based on data. So I think both the collection of data and the use of data to have these informed dialogues has been a total revolution in communication.

Who inspired you most along the way – marketing theorists or practitioners?

I think it was the latter. In the early days, I worked with a man named Casper Pinsker who ran a New York-based mail order advertising agency. Though he probably did not gain recognition in the annals of marketing, he did have a dialogue sense. That is, his advertisers all used coupons and did want to hear from consumers.

Then, of course, I went to Maxwell Sackheim who'd recently opened his own agency. He had trained at Sears Roebuck and was an extraordinary copywriter. He had an acute ear for the consumer and I think I learned much of what I know from him. He was a hard taskmaster – a difficult man with a great temper – but also possessing great intelligence. And he really forced me to become what I am, because otherwise I would have gotten lost somewhere in the pack. I think I would have been fired. As a matter of fact, I know so. The only way I saved myself each time was by coming up with an idea.

Why did you decide to set up your own agency?

I was 38 years old, and was the best-known young executive in this growing field of direct response advertising. Most people thought I was Max's partner, but in fact I owned no shares in the agency. I had regularly received other job offers, but hadn't been interested. I loved my work, but at that time didn't love my job.

I wasn't driven by money or power, but a realization that it was time to rethink. I felt ready for the freedom to follow my own vision. And that meant I would have to resign. Some of my colleagues joined me, and we set up Wunderman, Ricotta & Kline in a hotel room. We had to start from scratch. In my autobiography, I describe it as adopted house cats that have suddenly been put back into the alley. But when one of my large clients decided to move the account to our new agency, we knew we would be okay.

What were the major challenges you faced in trying to promote good direct marketing over the years?

I think the major challenge I faced was that direct marketing was unknown. The challenge was to make it a major marketing discipline that was known and practised, had a recognized impact and was governed by rules. If my contribution to the industry has meant anything, it's to have made direct marketing a key factor in advertising. Previously it didn't exist, although there was general advertising and assorted fragments of direct mail, mail order and so on.

The sea change came with a speech I made back in 1973 at the Massachusetts Institute of Technology (MIT). If others found it effective, I found it a revelation. I remember when writing it that I was challenged by the idea that such an august institution, which was inviting marketing professors from all the other universities around Boston, including Harvard, had invited me to make this speech about what I did. Suddenly I realized that I couldn't just mumble. I couldn't digress. How should I address this concept? I had to name it, I had to define it, I had to describe what it did, what it had done.

Was that the first time you'd actually had to put it in those terms?

I'd made a lot of speeches before, but none of the groups I'd addressed before were as challenging as this one. And, you know, Senator Vance Hartke of Indiana entered it into the congressional record: finally, direct marketing had official recognition.

My own contribution, I think, was to influence the Direct Mail Association. I argued that it was following an archaic and limited discipline and had to become the Direct Marketing Association (DMA) if it was to grow. And I think it was I, more than anybody, who forced that change.

Did you have a sense that you were a pioneer?

Yes, I always had a sense that I was pioneering. I mean, I grew up in tough times and faced tough problems and one had to initiate ideas and solve problems to survive. But the idea of solving problems is always thrilling, exciting and when you've got one down, it's an amazing moment. And to this day, if I write a phrase or think a thought, I still get as excited as I did when I was a kid.

When you were first promoting direct marketing, who was listening?

I made it my business to speak to a lot of audiences and there was an awful lot of nodding going on. I didn't know whether that meant anything – whether my ideas were penetrating or if people were simply nodding in agreement. In some countries, they were nodding because they were asleep. But in addressing groups, my main aim was to keep them awake and interested and hope that the nods were really based on the impact that it was having on them.

When you went into companies, did you have a sense that it was easier to get your message across to the chief executive officer (CEO), say, than to the marketing director?

I've always felt that the CEO represents, not the tactics of the company, but its philosophy. So if direct marketing was to be adopted, it had to be strategic rather than tactical. To be strategic, it had to have the consent and support of the CEO. So my target was always the CEO.

What was the reaction from other parts of the market?

Well, what happened originally was that other media worried about us. We were faced with not just antipathy, which would have been okay, but hostility, which wasn't. They thought we were going to eat their lunch and, of course, we weren't. We were using media in a more relevant way and I can't think of any medium that has since become obsolete. The strange thing is that outdoor advertising is still there and effective, and radio, too. They've all found a way to proceed into the future and they're all viable, and what I like so much is that, like a painter, our palette is full of colours.

Do you think that growth and consolidation over the years has led to a lack of creativity or a lessening of creativity in the marketing services arena?

I don't think that's true. In my time, there were a few extraordinary, creative people and we knew exactly who they were and what they did. Today, however, what you have is like a giant fleet, a flotilla of direct marketing companies, all with staff who do a good job. I think it's so much easier today to have access to the right kind of expertise for learning and from a wider variety of sources than ever before. Plus, there's the fact that direct marketing is now respected.

There was a time, early in my life, when if someone at a cocktail party asked what I did and I told them direct marketing – well, they'd laugh at me. Now, if I go to any gathering the same answer is likely to provoke respect. And that's true for all practitioners. We don't have to suffer being some kind of second-rate part of advertising any more.

> *There was a time, early in my life, when if someone at a cocktail party asked what I did and I told them direct marketing – well, they'd laugh at me. Now, if I go to any gathering the same answer is likely to provoke respect. And that's true for all practitioners. We don't have to suffer being some kind of second-rate part of advertising any more.*

Do you think that one of the reasons that direct marketing has gained such prestige is because this is now an age of measurement, and CEOs find it very accountable compared to, say, advertising?

We are totally accountable, which is a great challenge. It's also a great reward. The fact is, we know what succeeds. If we're good at it, we keep experimenting and testing things until we get the most effective commercial advertisement, letter or whatever, that we're capable of because of measurement. Other forms of measurement of general advertising are not, I think, quite that precise. We can count, we can say this thing did x%, or this thing did x plus a certain percent – and you can't do that in general advertising. You can discriminate between successful and less than successful advertising, but not as accurately, not as precisely.

In your view, should a response mechanism be built into all general advertising now?

Well, there are always going to be two forms of advertising. One is about creating impressions and attitudes, the other about creating responses and specific information. I think general advertising is attitudinal, and while we use attitudinal material, we are not so interested in the attitudinal result. We want physical material result. We want a sale, an enquiry or some other visible indication that we have been effective.

The internet is now an integral part of marketing. How did you view it at the start?

I think the internet is obviously the most accountable of media. I worked early on with the people at both MIT and California Institute of Technology when the internet was called the Arpanet, and viewed as an academic tool used by both the military and academicians. I was involved in its inception, and gradually we saw the development from the Arpanet to the internet, which involved the wide public. The Arpanet, however, was a kind of experimental laboratory tool that led to what we have now, the widespread influence of the internet here and abroad. As an aside, I read about China and the problems caused by its imposition of censorship and the difficulty of doing so. It's interesting.

What did your growing association with the internet stem from?

I think it was because some of the speeches I made at the time were to audiences that contained people of influence in both industry and academia. This was particularly true when I spoke at major universities and enabled me to become friends with, say, Nicholas Negroponte who was so influential at MIT, and Peter Drucker likewise. Peter and I spoke on the same platforms time and time again and we always compared notes and kind of taught each other.

How did you view its potential?

I can't claim to having had a vision of its eventual popularity, but I had an absolute fascination with its potential. I knew what it could do, was using it, and viewing it as a technological miracle that could bring life to the kind of dreams I had about dialogues between consumers and advertisers. I didn't forecast that it would become as popular as it has, but I certainly knew it was vitally important.

Who would you say are the main marketing influencers and visionaries of today?

I think our own person here, Daniel Morel, Wunderman's chairman and CEO, has organized this agency into a very effective instrument in the use of data and relevant communication. He even looks to have done so more efficiently than perhaps anybody has before. So I look to him. And then, of course, I have some friends like Howard Draft. He's certainly been a wonderful competitor and I think he's done good work. Ogilvy & Mather, whatever it takes on, has also been effective. They've always been efficient competitors and I respect them all.

Current views of marketing

What's the current problem that's taxing your brain?

Well, I think it's the empowerment of the consumer. It's what I call the great dialogue, the fact that finally there's no longer one-way speech between the consumer and the advertiser. It's an increasingly important dialogue where the advertiser will have to, if he hasn't already, install a kind of listening department because in the past the advertising department was always something that spoke.

Now, a listening department is important because consumers are certainly more outgoing, while media, such as the internet, make dialogue possible. In the past, we've had things like return prepaid postage and the 800 number, which enabled crude consumer messages to get back to the advertiser, but nothing like the internet existed where an actual real-time dialogue could take place.

If you look at the current challenges facing marketers, are they failing to press ahead with the advertiser/consumer dialogue?

No, I think that dialogue is happening. I think we're seeing a whole lift in the process. There are always backward companies who take longer to get the truth than others, but there are also always CEOs and marketing directors who are sharper. I think on the whole, though, there's a wave beginning to surge and I think it's large enough to even be called tidal. I wouldn't call it direct marketing, but I certainly would call it information-based relevant marketing.

Increasingly, if I were to use one word to define the nature of today's marketing dialogue, it's a matter of 'relevance'. It isn't just saying something to everybody; it's the attempt to try to say a thing of the moment. The ideal is to send the right message to the right person at the right time. This would be perfection, assuming that there's an advertising heaven to which a few of us will get.

And the fragmentation in communications really doesn't dilute relevance. As a matter of fact, it makes it so much more essential. Increasingly, if I were to use one word to define the nature of today's marketing dialogue, it's a matter of 'relevance'. It isn't just saying something to everybody; it's the attempt to try to say a thing of the moment. The ideal is to send the right message to the right person at the right time. This would be perfection, assuming that there's an advertising heaven to which a few of us will get.

How close are we to this advertising heaven?

In an information and database world, we're getting closer to the right thing and the right person. We're not getting a lot closer to the right time, because only the consumer knows what that is. And unless the consumer initiates the transaction, the right time is the lost instrument.

Is another problem that the right time is such a fleeting moment?

Absolutely.

What particular impact do you think the internet is having?

The internet offers a quick price comparison, instead of people having to visit many stores and make their own comparisons. There was a good article on the front page of the *Wall Street Journal* about Chinese consumers overwhelming retailers with team tactics. They're forming groups on the internet, finding each other there, and arranging to go to a retailer as a gaggle.

Once there, they demand a discount. One says: 'Oh, we want about 20 automobiles. And for that number we want a 30% discount.' It's an absolutely new use of the computer. Chinese computer use is quite sophisticated anyway, but here you see people forming buying groups to apply pressure on retailers. In other words, it's the consumer dictating the price rather than the retailer. It's revolutionary.

So do you think that the balance of power will ultimately shift worldwide?

Will it happen here? Who knows? One thing about the internet is that it attracts clusters of people, groups with similar interests. In the USA I'm not aware that it attracts groups with similar interests in the purchase of products. But it is in China, the ultimate bargaining society. The Chinese have always been sharp consumers. Now, as I said, they're banding together on the internet and then 35 or 40 of them are going into a retailer and saying: 'We want to buy 40 of your products and, therefore, we demand the following terms.' That's an absolutely new phenomenon.

There are also sites that allow consumers to design their own tool parts at a distance, which are then made for them in the Far East. What impact would you see sites like these having on marketing?

I think that's a long-term trend anyway. What will happen is that product modification is going to be part of service: when you get beyond price, you have to get into service. There's an absolute minimum to price. You can't sell below cost, but there is no maximum on service. The offering of services will, I think, continue to increase. I'm unsure whether American or European consumers will do what the Chinese have done, but I think the pressure for service is growing in our Western societies.

In the past, you've said that you could envisage a time when people would sign up with, say, a Colgate-Palmolive, to provide all their dental products, services and toothbrushes and toothpaste. Do you think this is a realistic view of the future?

I must admit to failure. I thought that was a good idea – consumers signing long-term contracts with advertisers – and that it would have occurred to somebody other than to me. I envisaged that advertisers such as Procter & Gamble or others would form similar clubs, using the internet as the perfect marketing and communications medium. It hasn't happened yet. Hopefully, eventually, it will.

Would you see the relationship that certain retailers have with consumers, say the one that Tesco has in the UK, as going part way towards realizing your futuristic dreams?

Absolutely right. I've read about the Tesco work. I think as competition gets keener and as the internet becomes more broadly used, then it begins to be thought of as strategic rather than tactical. I think a lot of the changes will evolve because people will learn what Tesco is doing and I think others are going to do the same.

Are there any other companies that stand out in your mind as practising information-based relevant marketing?

Well, just look at the client list of our company. They wouldn't be there otherwise. They've got what they wanted. They didn't come here for a jingle.

Would you care to highlight any of them?

Well, even though I don't serve specific clients these days, Microsoft is perhaps one whom I find terribly exciting. I think there's real compatibility between the pair of us: we both recognize and have the same vision of the future, but that's not to say that we don't have that with other clients. I want to be very careful to point out that we serve all of our clients with equal fervour.

Are there any myths about marketing that you'd like to see dispelled?

There are people who say they're doing information-based dialogue marketing, but I think there are a lot of myths involved. They may believe what they're saying, but I think the practice is not uniform and there aren't that many companies at the frontline. But, as always, you have echelons. You have the best, the second best, the mediocre and the poor and that's as true of this industry as any other.

What is your slant on the public view of junk mail, and call centres, which people feel are intrusive?

The phrase 'junk mail' was not originated by the public, but by the competition. I think people like to receive mail. I mean, unless an advertiser is absolutely stupid or inept, if your name is on the outside of an envelope there should be something relevant inside it.

I recognize that there are all levels of skill in our industry and a lot of people who still haven't learned how to do it. I used to have a collection, an ill-fated hall of the irrelevant. When I made speeches one of the ways I got attention was to read some of the mail addressed to me just to get my point over. That said, if you do it wrong, then you're doing yourself harm. The necessity of becoming expert and apt is terribly important.

What do you think about the use of these techniques in the political arena?

Well, good politicians listen. Take polling: how much of politics today and how much of policy is a result of polling? All good politicians have to poll the public because they're interested in getting votes in the same way that an advertiser is interested in getting sales. A vote is a kind of sale.

I think that political advertisers are increasingly using more sophisticated forms of research and listening to understand – not just what the general public is feeling, but also the feelings of individuals. Increasingly, I get mail from my local politicians addressed to me and relating to something I've either written about or they've polled me on. I also think that the nature of politics will again become more personal as it was in the early days when politicians knew their constituents. Those who choose not to will do so at their own risk. I think they're going to be forced to do so and to represent what their constituents want.

What advice would you give somebody starting off in this industry who wants to learn?

There are so many ways to learn, so many good books. I think anybody entering this industry has to study it as you would any other. What's interesting is that it's open to study. It's an industry that makes itself accessible. We have an increasing number of universities doing a bang-up job of teaching direct marketing as part of their marketing program.

If a young person asked me today how to succeed in direct marketing – assuming that they have the wit for success but not necessarily the tools – I would answer that there are so many good universities, marketing courses and teachers out there that one could attend any number of establish-ments and get a first-class basic education in marketing. I think that's fundamental.

The DMA, meanwhile, does an excellent job of collecting and making available materials, while there is any number of good speakers and sessions/assemblies that are constantly accessible. I don't speak that often any more, though I get a lot of invites, because I feel to a degree I'm repeat-ing myself. And that doesn't necessarily excite me.

Beyond that, I think attendance at seminars and finally getting a job with a firm where you can get some experience is vital. Nowadays there are so many. The fact is, in my time you couldn't find one. I was lucky. I found Maxwell Sackheim, one of the few people who wrote that kind of copy, but I didn't have an alternative. Well no, to be fair, there was one other called Schwab & Beatty at that point. But if I hadn't got a job with either of these, I would have had no way of learning direct marketing unless, of course, I went to an advertiser.

Getting more personal

What do you think it was about you as a person that made you go down the route you have chosen?

I was born and grew up in a time of prosperity, but I reached maturity at a time of depression. In other words, I was born in 1920 and, by the time I was 11 or 12, I was acutely aware of the fact that my friends' fathers were losing their jobs. Mine had died when I was nine. I saw men seeking work of any kind and the future looked dim and glum indeed.

To survive I had to be competitive. I also, when tested, turned out to have a good IQ. I was known to be bright. I was promoted, I was two years ahead of my time at school and they kept pushing me forward. I'm not sure that I benefited, but I was the runt among the big guys, because they kept pushing me into these classes.

When I was in high school you graduated at 18, but I graduated before I was 16. So I looked around and everybody else had long reached puberty. Yet here I was, this kid with the squeaky voice. I wasn't tall and though I was a good athlete, I didn't excel at brawny sports. Still, I was quick.

You obviously had a competitive streak from early on?

Well, at one point, I was a world-class table tennis player. I was competitive at sports. I grew up very near Yankee Stadium. In those days, the great players like Babe Ruth and others used to come down and coach us kids who were playing baseball and inspire us to want to be better.

I lived near a public park that had tennis courts and a baseball field and all that. And I used to watch these highly skilled professionals and try to learn. Then I became friends with the American champion ping-pong champion and he and I travelled and gave exhibitions together. So I was an exhibition table tennis player at one point in my life. I was competitive and I always wanted to learn and wanted to excel.

With ping-pong you have to be very quick on your feet. Did this show through in the ideas you came up with?

I think I was quick in general. I don't know how deep my intellect was, but I certainly was quick as a learner.

Do you have what you consider a defining moment of your life when something happened and you said, 'Yes, I know now this is where I'm going'?

I think the defining moment was when I kind of sequestered myself and wrote that MIT speech. It was then I understood that I wasn't dealing with a tactic, a trick or a promotion – I was dealing with a fundamental change in how marketing was developing. Suddenly, I went from being a tactician to a strategist and not just that:

I think the defining moment was when I kind of sequestered myself and wrote that MIT speech. It was then I understood that I wasn't dealing with a tactic, a trick or a promotion – I was dealing with a fundamental change in how marketing was developing. Suddenly, I went from being a tactician to a strategist and not just that: an advocate and a missionary. I simply had come upon what I knew my life's work was going to be.

an advocate and a missionary. I simply had come upon what I knew my life's work was going to be.

You have for a long time been a keen collector of Dogon art from Africa. Did going to that continent influence your approach to work?

Oh, did it ever! Because what you try to do there is reach a consensus. This process means that the wise men sit in kind of a thatched roof shelter, they pose a philosophical problem and then try to reach a consensus. Even when you buy things, you bargain. Everything involves haggling. So in the marketplace, if you think about it, the haggling is really an attempt to reach a consensus between the buyer and the seller. It was that desire to achieve consensus that was such a strong motivation.

What was your proudest moment?

I think I'm proudest of the fact that this agency, with its offices all over the world and its 4,000 smart employees, has my name on it. We operate in so many languages, so many venues and in so many countries. And for many people the name 'Wunderman' stands for global direct marketing. Also, the influence we have had on the marketing system of the world gives me great pleasure and pride. I come in here every day and see things on the wall that I've either said or written and I just take great pride in that.

Selected publication

Being Direct: Making Advertising Pay, Direct Marketing Association, 1996, 2004.

Index

Index compiled by Annette Musker